THE HEALTH ZODIAC

A Practical Guide
to Understanding
Your Health Cycles
Through Astrology

PAMELA ROWE

ASHGROVE PRESS, BATH

THE HEALTH ZODIAC

First published in Great Britain by
Ashgrove Press Limited
4 Brassmill Centre, Brassmill Lane
Bath BA1 3JN
and distributed in the USA by
Avery Publishing Group Inc.
120 Old Broadway
Garden City Park, New York 11040

Originally published by Interface,
NSW, Australia

ISBN 1-85398-039-0

Printed and bound in Great Britain by
The Cromwell Press,
Broughton Gifford, Wilts

Dedication

This book is dedicated to my husband of two marriages, Howard, and my two daughters Michele and Angela, for their untiring patience.

Biography

1970   Commenced study of astrology
1977   Commenced work as a full-time astrology lecturer and consultant.
1980 – 1989   Lecturer in Astrology, Council of Adult Education, Melbourne Australia
1984   Founded the Australian Academy of Astrology & Cosmobiology

MEMBERSHIPS

Fellow and Professional Member of the Federation of Australian Astrologers
Member of the American Federation of Astrologers
Lectured at International Astrology Conferences throughout Australia, New Zealand and the USA

WRITING

Articles and research on astrology published in Australia, USA and Germany
In 1981 article on Kidney Disease Research was published in an Australian Medical Journal
Currently astrological writer for *Perth Weekly Times* and *Nature & Health* Magazine

MEDIA

2 years resident astrologer 'Good Morning Melbourne', Channel 10 Melbourne
A weekly segment for 2 years with Radio 3AW Melbourne
4 years scripting and recording 'Dial-a-Horoscope' for Telecom Australia, broadcast nationally, daily.

Contents

Introduction and acknowledgements

In true synchronistic fashion, astrology became a major force in my life in 1970, the year of my divorce from my husband Howard. As a single mother, there was time to investigate and discover myself. Doris Greaves, my first astrology teacher, came into my life at this time and several years later Doris examined my work for accuracy, after which I began to practise professionally.

The truth of astrology is a fire which burns within and one's first teacher can illuminate or eliminate that flame. The astrology teacher who fans the interest holds a special place in the heart and Doris' love of astrology left an indelible mark in my life. Although I had been following astrology and studying it as a lay person since I was a child of nine, I did not realise that one could actually become an astrologer in Australia until I met Doris Greaves.

The longer I studied astrology, the more I understood the different perspectives which existed between myself and my ex-husband, and how the relationship had developed at the worst possible time. Whilst astrology cannot accept the credit for age and experience, it played an important role in the re-establishment of our relationship and subsequent re-marriage many years later.

Since then my purpose has been to make accessible to as many people as possible, the help and encouragement offered by astrology, so that they may be helped as I was helped. This I have done through consultations and astrology classes. Many thousands of pupils have passed through my classes since 1977, and in 1984 I established the Australian Academy of Astrology and Cosmobiology. To date, the crowning achievement of my teaching years was in 1988, when blind student Ramona Stewart mastered this highly complex and visual study. Details of my methods of teaching astrology to the blind were published in Australia and the United States in 1989.

Medicine and astrology were once historically aligned faculties, but are today scientifically removed from each other. My own interest in health and medicine included eight years working in a teaching hospital, which gave me a great respect for the dedication I witnessed there. But for those versed in astrology, the connection between lowered resistance, serious illness and recurring astrological patterns to coincide with these health conditions, is undeniable.

Twenty years of consistent astrological findings cannot be shrugged off as coincidence. Astrology has nothing to do with blind faith. Ethically practised, it can give people hope and confidence to love themselves as they actually are. It is not a religion and should not be practised as such, or treated as such by those who have a limited knowledge of it. It is a subjective science and like any subject dealing with human nature, its success or failure depends upon those practising it.

The complexity of the technical side of astrology makes it difficult to present it in its abbreviated Sun sign form, which is so popular with the public. In this book I have included the popular format, but have endeavoured to open the door of understanding a bit wider by explaining a few advanced techniques in simple language. Here is knowledge which you can use in your own lives.

I wish to acknowledge my astrology students and clients, whose feedback has been essential to the accurate testing of astrological theories. Some of my own findings may be controversial, but they will encourage new avenues of thought and help keep the astrological spiral in motion. To single out and acknowledge individual astrologers is difficult, because there are so many in Australia, New Zealand and the United States who have been inspiring and supportive — and to these people I offer special thanks. The American medical astrologer Mary Vohryzek, believed in the wholistic approach to life. She left a lasting professional and personal impression and is sadly missed in the astrological world today.

The mystique of good and bad health has always been a special interest of mine. To maintain equilibrium and sound health under extreme and complex circumstances, I believe we must listen to our higher self and if possible, act on it. With the advent of a pending physical and emotional crisis in my life in 1985, the force of synchronicity closed one door and threw open another — figure skating. This poetry on ice offered a high energy expression at a low ebb in my life. Here was an opportunity to practise what I preached and test many theories. Thanks to the generosity and expertise of my coach Trevor Bussey, I became stronger and healthier than ever before. There is a kindred spirit among skaters, which I am sure also exists in other sports — a remarkable force which entered my life at exactly the right moment — Synchronicity is covered in more detail in Chapter 1.

The art work and lettering for this book is by Rick Anderson. Kevin Schache of Astrogenetics Research provided the horoscope computer charts and helped me with the research. Rick and Kevin are from Melbourne, Australia and I thank them both for their enthusiasm and assistance. And finally a special acknowledgement to my friends of the New Age, who are working in their own spiritual way to help humanity and make this planet a better place for creative living.

PAMELA J. ROWE
September 1989

'A human being is a part of the whole called by us as universe, a part limited in time and space. He experiences himself, his thoughts and feelings as something separated from the rest, a kind of optical delusion of his consciousness. This delusion is a kind of prison for us, restricting us to our personal desires and to affection for a few persons nearest to us. Our task must be to free ourselves from this prison by widening our circle of compassion to embrace all living creatures and the whole of Nature in its beauty.'

— *Albert Einstein* —

Chapter One

Astrology and Medicine — The Pioneers

Since the dawn of humanity, the heavens have provided a continual fascination for the enquiring mind. Five thousand years ago in Mesopotamia, it was believed that angry gods and evil spirits created disease and that it was a cosmic condition. People observed the every-changing planetary cycles and adapted their lifestyles to suit the seasons. Their observations were interwoven with superstition, religion and magic and it was from this foundation that the diagnosis and cure of illness was based — the medicine man of the tribe was held in awe, an attitude inherited by later generations. It is only in recent years that the modern medicine man has emerged as a friendly and helpful, albeit scientific individual.

During this early period in history the desire to 'drive illness from the body' was formulated. Variations of the theme included cutting holes in the skull of the patient to release evil spirits, headaches and mental illness. In later years cold and heat treatments, herbs, poisons and blood-letting were popular practices. These days dangerous drugs are used to drive illnesses from the body. When researching ancient and modern medicine, one frequently discovers two schools of thought — those who wish to eliminate the final effects of illness and those who wish to prevent illness.

In ancient Greece, faith healing was a natural part of daily life. Sick people gathered in temples and churches built to honour Asclepius, the Greek God of Healing. From approximately 3000 BC great medical progress was made by the Egyptians: the Egyptian physician Imhotep (2700 BC), was revered as a god. Illustrations of Asclepius and Imhotep depict them holding a stick with a snake entwined around it and the illustration of the stick and snake is still used today as a symbol of the medical profession.

Former men of science such as the Greek physician Hippocrates (460–377 BC), known as the Father of Medicine, were well versed in astrology. In the days when a physician was not considered competent unless he could interpret the horoscope of his patient, Hippocrates was the first physician to separate medicine from religious superstition and to practise it as a science and art. The Hippocratic Oath, named for him, is a code of ethics still recited by many newly graduating medical students which enhances confidentiality, ideals and integrity in the practice of medicine.

Hippocrates believed that correct diet and a relaxed environment were important pre-requisites to successful healing. He concentrated on improving the habits and living conditions of his patients and maintained that human nature was the physician of disease. Hippocrates refused to administer strong drugs unless they had been thoroughly tested and he was satisfied they would prove beneficial to his patients. (His favourite diet for his patients was barley gruel and his favourite medicine was honey.) He theorised that through the controlling effect of the glands, an imbalance of the body humours (blood, phlegm, black bile and yellow bile), would result in pain and disease.

Galen (AD 130–200) linked the four humours with four temperaments — Choleric (quick-tempered), Phlegmatic (sluggish), Sanguine (bouyant) and Melancholic (dejected). Today modern thinking accepts that an imbalance of glandular functions can relate to temperament. The Greeks associated the humours with the four elements — Fire, Earth, Air and Water. The Choleric humour was linked to the Fire signs Aries, Leo and Sagittarius; the Phlegmatic humour was linked to the Earth signs Taurus, Virgo and Capricorn; the Sanguine humour was linked to the Air signs Gemini, Libra and Aquarius; and the Melancholic humour was linked to the Water signs Cancer, Scorpio and Pisces.

Paracelsus (1493–1541) was born in Switzerland and received his early training in medicine and chemistry from his father, who was a physician and chemist. Paracelsus believed that 'everything in the heavens can be found in Man, only differing in form and substance'. He was a profound thinker who theorised that a person possessed three bodies — the physical body (carnal), the sidereal/planetary body (soul) and the luminous body (spirit). Infectious disease and negative planetary influences could lead to illness in the physical and sidereal bodies. But it would take negative emotions such as rage, torment and hatred to damage the third body of the spirit, which would result in the manifestation of physical illness. Many people confirm the theory of Paracelsus as highly relevant; some call it psychosomatic illness.

Englishman William Harvey (1578–1657) is best remembered for his work on the blood circulation of the body, publishing 'An Anatomical Treatise on the Motion of the Heart and Blood in Animals' in 1628.

Ambroise Pare (1510–1590) was the founder of modern surgery. To dress wounds, Pare used egg yolk, oil of roses and turpentine in preference to boiling oil, which was the standard treatment at the time.

Nicholas Culpeper was a famous 17th century medical astrologer and physician who further developed the work of Paracelsus. He specialised in herbal remedies and linked the healing properties of plants and herbs to the planets and zodiac signs. Many of Culpeper's cures are still popular and *The Simmonite-Culpeper Herbal Remedies* is a valuable addition to the library of those seeking the natural way. A typical Culpeper remedy to appeal to the stressed and overworked woman is the herb rosemary, which is attributed to 'the Sun in the celestial sign Aries, and therefore good for nervous headaches, tremblings and female complaints'.

In 1676, amateur Dutch scientist Anton van Leeuwenhoek created a new perspective in medical research when he used the microscope to study certain microbes.

Edward Jenner administered the first vaccination for smallpox to a small boy named James Phipps in 1796. Ether anesthesia was publicly administered for the first time in Massachusetts General Hospital in 1846 by American dentist William Morton.

During the 1800s the great scientist Louis Pasteur (1822–1895) made significant milestones in his research into the areas of bacteria, disease-immunity and vaccination. Pasteur has an exceptional horoscope, which is not surprising when considering his exceptional life and achievements — it is interpreted in Chapter 4.

And so the list of inspiring medical pioneers grows. Florence Nightingale, the founder of modern nursing, was born in Florence, Italy on 12 May, 1820, while her British parents were living abroad. Through the sheer strength of her character and courage, Florence generated worldwide reform in nursing techniques and hospital administration during her lifetime. Even as a child she was remarkable in her motivation to care for the sick and underprivileged, especially when we reflect on what was expected of a woman of her era, born into a rich family. Like all great pioneers, she was ahead of her time.

Florence was born soon after the new Moon, when the Sun and Moon were in conjunction in the sign of Taurus. Anyone born at the time of the new Moon has a tendency to be single-minded (see Chapter 5, 'The Moon Phases and Personality Traits'), but the new Moon in the fixed sign of Taurus reinforces and magnifies this trait. Mercury, the planet of communication, was in the dynamic sign of Aries; Virgo, the sign of service and perfectionism, was rising on the Ascendant. Naturally there are many other factors to consider when interpreting the chart; even with limited interpretation it can be seen that Florence had a great obsession to serve the less fortunate. Any resistance to her plans would be met with a fiery and determined response. There was no room in her nature to compromise her ideals. Students of astrology can examine the full horoscope of Florence Nightingale (Figure 1).

With the advent of the age of biochemistry, science and astrology drifted further apart. In many cases Astrology was thrown out of the window along with the superstitions and without a reasonable assessment of its potential. Could it be that the baby has been thrown out with the bathwater? There is little doubt that prescribing treatment or medication without qualifications and comprehensive knowledge of the human body is illegal and irresponsible. However, an interest in health and an observation of human illness cannot be similarly categorised.

In recent times there has been an enormous growth of interest in astrology in relation to its psychological and humanistic aspects. Psychiatrist and psychoanalyst Carl Jung (1875–1961), who was one of the great minds of the past century, made no secret of the fact that he used the horoscopes of his patients to assist in the diagnosis of their condition. He discovered that there were many similarities inherent in their horoscopes which coincided with specific character traits. His study of the horoscopes of marriage partners and their connecting features is well

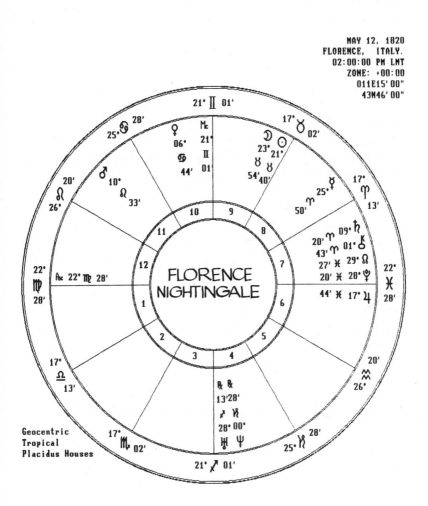

MAY 12, 1820
FLORENCE, ITALY.
02:00:00 PM LMT
ZONE: +00:00
011E15' 00"
43N46' 00"

Figure 1: *Florence Nightingale's Horoscope*

known and outlined in his work *Synchronicity: An Acausal Connecting Principle.* Jung's spirituality provided him with a broad canvas to expand the boundaries of existing knowledge.

His theory of Synchronicity links events through 'meaningful coincidence rather than causality'. This concept can be applied to astrology. We have all experienced 'meaningful coincidences' — the act of being in the right (or wrong) place at the right (or wrong) time. We interpret it as a psychic experience, a stroke of destiny of an act of God. The event may be a chance meeting, an accident, sickness or an insignificant, uncalculated action which activates a chain reaction and ultimately alters our destiny. Do you remember a time when you were desperately seeking the answer to a question within yourself when an unassociated person made a casual remark which you overhead and which answered your question? Or did you select a book from a shelf of hundreds, flip through the pages and recognise a revelationary answer to your problem, supplied by an author discussing an unrelated topic? The variations are endless. Religious texts tell us to 'seek and ye shall find' — the answers are all around us, waiting to be found when the time is right for us to recognise them. For what is of profound relevance to one person is of little importance to another.

Synchronicity often makes itself apparent during periods of crisis. An option may be closed to us, something is removed from our life, over which we have no control, forcing another door open and catapulting us onto a path we would never by choice have taken, a path which later proves to enhance our life and generate deep happiness.

It does not take long for those consistently involved with astrology to notice synchronicity at work. The placement of the planets in the heavens at the moment of a person's birth actually coincide with potential character traits which can be read, understood and developed positively. The application of astrological techniques can measure and compare life events or expressions and list them symbolically. Astrology does not interfere with the free will — people make choices — but every moment in time has a quality, a flavour which effects each of us in an individual way. This flavour and how it relates to the individual is the factor which can be measured by the astrologer. The outcome of the energies can only be speculated upon, the events cannot be predicted with total accuracy.

It seems to me that 'like attracts like'. Despite our basic characteristics, our lives are mentally, emotionally and physically in continual motion. The 'changeability' can be observed in the daily conditions of the activated horoscope. Whether people attract (what they interpret as) positive or negative experiences into their lives, will depend on what energies are being generated by them at the time. The question of a deliberate output of positivity and negativity is one factor; then there are the positive and negative astrological conditions prevailing. There seems to be a correlation between the two, despite the fact that there may be no conscious desire to attract difficult circumstances. But even positiveness and negativity are relative; what some people perceive as negative, others interpret as a learning experience. However, you will attract your own perspective of a positive life by adopting a positive attitude. You have the power and ability to modify what life offers you by neutralising your negatives and converting them into positives.

You may have noticed that the people who cross your path daily and the associated circumstances connecting them to your day often appear to have an ordered sequence. Perhaps on a specific day there are similarities in the type of people you meet or in their attitude towards you; perhaps you experience two or three events of a similar nature. An example of a 'positive sequence' involves Jane who in the one day received a raise in salary, met a long-lost friend in the street and had a proposal of marriage from someone she had loved for many years. An example of a 'negative sequence' involves Jerry, who in the one day lost a major work contract, received a letter in the mail from his fiance breaking off the engagement, and by evening was ill with the flu. Both days could happen to any one of us, but ask an astrologer for their interpretation of the events and they will immediately suggest several influences which could have been operating on the days in question.

There is no-one in a better position than a professional counsellor to test the theory of synchronicity. The counsellor may interview four clients or patients daily. Often the appointments are made by a secretary or reshuffled at short notice. As an astrologer I have found that there is frequently a common thread in the four horoscopes of those who cross my path in the one day; the common thread makes a link with my own activated horoscope. It is extraordinary. On some occasions three of the four are born on the same day or within a few days of each other.

Psychoanalyst and astrologer Liz Greene discusses synchronicity in depth in her book *The Astrology of Fate.* Dr Greene states: –

> *'Synchronous situations seem to flock like crows around astrological and analytical work. Perhaps this is because these fields require a constant encountering of a relationship with archetypal material and once one enters this archetypal "field" one rapidly becomes exposed to the strange way in which it seems to "order" both outer and inner events.'*

In his book *Synchronicity, The Bridge Between Matter and Mind,* F. David Peat pointed out that synchronicities are usually linked with periods of transformation such as 'births, deaths, falling in love, psychotherapy, intense creative work or a change of profession'.

Citing Jung's theory, David Peat stated

> *'… it is the nature of synchronicity to have meaning and, in particular, to be associated with a profound activation of energy deep within the psyche. It is as if the formation of patterns within the unconscious mind is accompanied by physical patterns in the outer world. In particular, as psychic patterns are on the point of reaching consciousness then synchronicities reach their peak; moreover, they generally disappear as the individual becomes consciously aware of a new alignment of forces within his or her personality.'*

One of my own thoughts on synchronicity is that the analyst, counsellor and astrologer continuously relate to people who are at major life crossroads. The adviser is reaching deep within his or her psyche to call upon personal training and experience in order to help the one in need of guidance. It is not surprising therefore , that such advisers observe an increase in synchronistic coincidences in their own day-to-day lives. The constant associations may help to trigger this mystic force.

COSMOBIOLOGY

Because my specialty training is in cosmobiology, I must include the important contribution made to medical astrology by the German astrologer Reinhold Ebertin (1901–1988), the founder of cosmobiology. During two trips to Europe I met Mr Ebertin and attended his conferences. His work in medical research is well documented in his books and articles. His system is precise, scientific and highly efficient for tabulating large numbers of cases of a specific type such as heart attacks or kidney disorders. Because he eliminated several esoteric factors, his work attracted the interest of scientific minds, and it will live on through the work of serious astrological researchers of the future.

THE GAUQUELIN RESEARCH

The most severe critics of astrology are usually those who have not taken the time to seriously research it. These are the ones who approach the subject with the biased attitude of 'How could it possibly work?'. The scientific feasibility of planetary consistencies existing at the time of birth of groups of individuals with a common factor, or of the planetary cycles effectively influencing our decision-making processes, often represents an unacceptable concept for the objective mind.

Michel Gauquelin, a French psychologist and scientist, has spent much of his life researching ancient astrological theories. As expected, he disproved many theories, but found some amazing consistencies which he could not discount. For example he spent years gathering exact birth particulars of large test groups of people in identical vocations, such as doctors, sports champions, politicians, scientists, writers, and actors. Gauquelin found unexpected consistencies beyond that expected of chance, in the rising and culminating planets at the moment of birth of those in the test groups. The fact that many of the children born to people in these groups shared similar planetary patterns at birth, raised the question of character traits and hereditary factors. Hereditary is discussed in more detail in Chapter 13.

Although Gauquelin denounced many ingrained traditional astrological beliefs, his work as a champion who has examined both sides of the story is admired and respected in astrological circles. Astrology students are well advised to examine the arguments against astrology along with its traditional concepts, in order to maintain order and balance. Those commencing studies are usually fired with an inner spark of knowledge, which they are hell-bent on confirming, often to the exclusion of all logical argument.

Gauquelin has written many books on his research and findings: *The Truth about Astrology, Cosmic Clocks* and *Birth Times* are three which I would recommend. In *The Truth about Astrology* he makes several radical statements, in particular that concerning the attitude of science to astrology.

> *'That some Chaldean priest could have had the notion, however crude, that the child at birth and the planets are "in sympathy"; that he could have glimpsed this true, yet "absurd", idea without the aid of statistics or a telescope; that he could have attributed aggressiveness and warfare to Mars with none of the tools of modern knowledge — all this defies belief'.*

He made a profound observation when he stated 'Scientists know that proof of planetary effects at birth would be equivalent in astrology to the Copernican revolution in astronomy (that the Earth was not the centre of the universe)'. This observation is borne out by history. The 'public image' of astrology is shackled to the abbreviated Sun sign version, which keeps the lid on its potential credibility. Sun sign astrology or 'fun astrology' is what the people want and it is what the people get. Facets of astrology which present themselves intelligently are often edited and played down. As Gauquelin points out ...

> *'The contemporaries of Copernicus stopped at nothing, not even crime, to keep the Earth at the centre of the universe, so crucial was it to their understanding of the universe and the destiny of man'.*

It is attitudes like these which label astrology with imaginary evil and prevent its fair appraisal. Like all things, astrology is only as good or evil as the person who practises it.

Remember the words of Ecclesiastes ...

> *To every thing there is a season, and a time to every purpose under heaven:*
> *A time to be born, and a time to die; a time to plant, and a time to pluck up to that which is planted;*
> *A time to kill, and a time to heal; a time to break down, and a time to build up;*

A time to weep, and a time to laugh; a time to mourn, and a time to dance;

A time to cast away stones, and a time to gather stones together; a time to embrace, and a time to refrain from embracing;

A time to get, and a time to lose; a time to keep, and a time to cast away;

A time to rend, and a time to sew; a time to keep silence, and a time to speak;

A time to love, and a time to hate; a time of war, and a time of peace.

Chapter Two

The Twelve Signs of the Zodiac
**Physical health and psychological manifestations.
An introduction**

PERSONAL ASTROLOGY

Personal astrology is based on the concept that we carry with us the qualities of a moment in time, in this case our birth moment — a little like the vintage of a good wine. A personal horoscope is a map of the heavens calculated for the time, date and place of birth, which is used by astrologers as a blueprint to indicate trends and potential in the life of that person. I liken the horoscope to a road map, which indicates the smooth and rocky areas of the life.

But the horoscope is incomplete. In itself, it does not include adequate information as to the child's genetic background, or the environmental factors into which the child was born. It consists of the planetary energies as they relate to each other, and determines which planets are rising, culminating or setting at the time of birth. Astrology discusses the energies themselves, but the individualised expression of the energies is variable. For example, a prince and a pauper may be born at the same time, in the same year in the same city. The expectations of each will be different, so that when the prince becomes a king, the pauper may finally become employed. Nevertheless, powerful people can rise from humble beginnings and a person with a powerful horoscope is recognised by the astrologer as having maximum life potential.

Specific areas of the complete horoscope relate to the health of the individual. Because this book is based predominately on Sun sign astrology, it has been necessary for me to approach the question of health from many different angles.

SUN SIGN ASTROLOGY

Sun sign astrology is an abbreviation of the comprehensive study of astrology. As the sun is in the same zodiac sign of the tropical zodiac at roughly the same time each year, it is one of the few con-

sistent factors available to astrologers who wish to present astrology to a public which is not familiar with astrology's technicali-
ties. But it is too simplistic to suppose that large groups of people
born within a few weeks of each other in any year, are going to
share common personality traits, career prospects and health
orientation, to name but a few of the claims made by Sun sign
astrology. Anyone doing serious research is bound to find
aggressive, sensitive, humanitarian, artistic and practical people
born under all signs of the zodiac. People who succeed and fail
are invariably born under all signs of the zodiac. So what is it that
maintains an almost universal interest in Sun sign astrology?

Firstly there is enough accuracy to keep Sun sign astrology
alive and well, even if it only caters for the casual observer and is
enjoyed for its entertainment value. It is a continual headache
for the serious astrologer writing a Sun sign column, to provide
adequate information without venturing beyond the Sun sign.
But the fact is, Sun sign astrologers may often be the only link to
the serious study of astrology.

Upon entering the Sun sign arena with the realisation that the
Arabians had used solar astrology comprehensively in the past, I
was surprised to discover some degree of accuracy in it. To sim-
plify its application, Sun sign astrology consists of calculating a
daily chart for each zodiac sign with the Sun placed in its rising
position on the horizon. It is based on the daily positions of the
planets in the heavens and their relationships to each other.
Much of it is symbolic and open to the interpretation of the
astrologer/writer. It stands to reason that as only a certain percentage of people are actually born at Sun rise, there will be far
more accuracy in some cases than others.

The truth about astrology is that we are actually what we
believe we are. Too much input about what we are supposed to
be like according to our zodiac sign, will defeat our purpose of
self-understanding and growth as an individual. Children who
grow up in a home where they are encouraged and praised for
their achievements are more likely to consider themselves suc-
cess-material than children who are continually criticised and
put down, or who have unreasonably high expectations placed
upon them by their parents. Sun sign astrology is a little like that
in that people can brainwash themselves with phantom qualities

or pre-judge their new acquaintances. I continually meet people who are reluctant to disclose their zodiac sign for fear of being pre-judged by its popular interpretation.

Keep in mind that what you read about your sign is partly historical, partly researched and partly coloured by the personal perspectives of the astrological writer. There are many good horoscope data text books on the market, for example *The American Book of Charts* and *Profiles of Women*, both by Lois M. Rodden. These are books of horoscopes of famous people born under all signs of the zodiac. It is a learning experience to study the charts of those who have achieved what you aspire to, and not rely on heresay. I guarantee you will be surprised and pleased.

In support of Sun sign astrology, I must add that astrologers have observed and tabled over a period of many centuries, the characteristics and potential of each zodiac sign. But as all signs have a positive and negative expression, there are no 'good' or 'bad' signs, but merely choices to be made as to how we express our positive and negative traits. Even the positiveness and negativity are subject to the perception of individual interpretation.

Personalised astrology is about variable perceptions, getting outside your own subjective viewpoint and understanding yourself and others. Under certain circumstances, as much as you expect your nearest and dearest ones to react in a similar manner to yourself, their perception of their environment and the world around them may be completely different to your own. They have the choice of denying their own individuality in order to conform with you, or alternatively rebelling against your standards. Either way, someone will be angry and disappointed — two dangerous factors in our quest for continuing good health.

SUN SIGN DATES

The dates I have listed for each zodiac sign are average dates. The reader may have noticed that the dates for the beginning and end of their zodiac sign often varies slightly, depending on the book or magazine referred to. The fact is that the changeover date for your zodiac sign can vary from year to year by approximately one day, so that both of the books or magazines you refer to would be correct for a particular year.

Born On the 'Cusp'

If a person is born on the dividing date between one zodiac sign and the next, he or she is said to be born on the cusp. If you were born on the cusp it is necessary for the astrologer to know the year and sometimes the time of your birth in order to establish which sign you were born under. Many astrologers believe that people born on the cusp take on the qualities of the two signs involved.

Psychological Traits of the Signs

The psychological attitude and physical health are closely linked. The mind is a powerful force and true spiritual harmony can do more for your health than any diet or wonder cure. In each zodiac sign interpretation I have included a few comments on the psychology of the sign, which may give a more wholistic health profile.

In his book *The Wisdom of Gibran: Aphorisms and Maxims,* Kahlil Gibran reminds us that 'We struggle to find life outside ourselves, unaware that the life we are seeking is within us.'

If we listened to our inner voice rather than the many 'experts' trading on our quest for enlightenment, our love of self and others would be enhanced and consequently our state of mental and physical well-being would improve.

All the zodiac signs have beautiful traits. The negative interpretations you have read relate to an over-abundance of a particular influence, which can sometimes create an imbalance. There are many helpful ways to compensate for what is lacking or excessive in ourselves. The most instinctive way is to attach ourselves to people who can supplement our lives with the qualities we lack, or alternatively to people who can draw upon our overload. Perhaps we should trust our primary psychic selves instead of analysing a relationship which we have become comfortable with, by attempting to place a negative slant on the differences which attracted us in the first place.

The Yin and Yang Signs

As a group, half of the zodiac signs are recognised as being more masculine, active and Yang than others. The other half are recognised as being more feminine, passive and Yin.

The Yang signs of the zodiac are Aries, Gemini, Leo, Libra, Sagittarius and Aquarius. These are the Fire and Air signs. People born under Yang signs are more likely to externalise their life expressions.

The Yin sings of the zodiac are Taurus, Cancer, Virgo, Scorpio, Capricorn and Pisces. These are the Earth and Water signs. People born under Yin signs are more likely to internalise their life expressions.

Such categorisation is a highly simplistic method of analysing the energy forces, but it is one which is readily understood. Although people born under Yang signs may feel they have more in common with other Yang signs, they can learn alternative modes of life expression from people born under Yin signs. The same applies to the Yin signs. Yin and Yang signs can help each other to grow. For more on mixing and matching the signs, see the section on 'The Qualities and Elements' in Chapter 4.

The ever-changing planetary patterns in the heavens can sometimes demonstrate an overload of Yin or Yang energy at the moment of birth, making it more difficult for some people than others to maintain their equilibrium. The degree of Yin or Yang in each individual can be determined through examining the full twelve points of the birth horoscope. In Chapter 12, 'The Onset of Illness', I have expanded the theory further, using examples of health conditions.

SIGN POLARITIES AND REFLEX ACTION THROUGH THE OPPOSITE SIGN
Each zodiac sign is linked to its opposite sign through a reflex action. Your opposite sign is the mirror image of your personality, so that many people over-compensate what is lacking in themselves through expressing their opposite polarity. This rule applies especially to health conditions. In the interpretation of each sign I have included a section on your sign polarity and how it relates to your health and well-being.

ARIES IS OPPOSITE TO LIBRA
TAURUS IS OPPOSITE TO SCORPIO
GEMINI IS OPPOSITE TO SAGITTARIUS
CANCER IS OPPOSITE TO CAPRICORN
LEO IS OPPOSITE TO AQUARIUS
VIRGO IS OPPOSITE TO PISCES.

Human beings are complex creatures. It is not feasible to presume that all people can be simply and neatly categorised into twelve packages labelled 'Zodiac Signs'. The study of your opposite polarity is your first experience in expanding your astrological horizons.

Chapter Three

The Twelve Signs of the Zodiac
Physical health and psychological manifestations. Interpretation

$\mathcal{V}$ARIES: 21 MARCH TO 20 APRIL

The symbol of Aries shows the head and spiralling horns of the ram, symbolic of the dynamic and positive energy associated with the sign. Aries is a cardinal Fire sign, denoting ambition, enterprise, impulse, urgency and adventure. Challenge is a magnet; easy game will quickly prove boring. The qualities of self-will and independence makes Aries people better leaders than followers.

Aries is ruled by Mars, the planet of initiative and aggression. It is interesting how the link between the sign and the planet so accurately describes the classical Arien type. Mars is the red planet. Perhaps the expression 'seeing red', to describe a fit of temper, originated from an association with Mars. Have you ever noticed how many Ariens are attracted to red cars and clothing? Not all Ariens of course, but noticeably more than chance. Those born under the sign of Aries should take special note of the section on Mars cycles in Chapter 6.

It is important for those endowed with the Aries spirit to externalise their energies. Internalised aggression can result in frustration, anger and ultimately deep depression, and it is frustrating for Ariens to play the passive/aggressive personality. Physical expressions such as sport, dance and the regenerating power of the great outdoors will provide spiritual nourishment for the depleted Arien.

Aries rules the head, cerebrum and motor centres of the brain. It is also associated with blood and muscle. Aries generates heat, so that fevers and inflammations are common, but the recuperative powers are good. Many of the Arien complaints can be attributed to the Arien nature. A strong appetite for life, combined with a pioneering spirit, can lead to over-commitment, complete with headaches, high blood pressure and stress. Impatience and urgency will induce the likelihood of accidents;

Ariens in too much of a hurry to eat at a leisurely pace are likely to suffer from malabsorption of nutrients, and later more severe digestive disturbances. Not in the habit of wasting time, their 'hit and run' approach to toilet habits does not improve the situation.

Psychologically, Aries people usually present as spontaneous, enthusiastic and generous. Their unusually high level of independence means that they rarely see the advantage of delegating work and responsibility to others. As a result many Ariens end up with their fingers in too many pies, driving themselves to excess and scattering their energy resources. Ariens are happiest when they achieve a harmonious balance of their energies and aggressions. Unfortunately it often takes a dramatic life crisis for them to take stock of their personal situation.

The Aries aggressiveness will externalise if it becomes necessary for them to forsake their individuality and bend to the will of others, which incidentally is quite rare. As mentioned above, blocked or disguised aggression can manifest in alternative channels; this is why some Ariens adopt a passive demeanour and appear to be less aggressive than they actually are.

In love, the Arien is an ardent lover, as bold and passionate in love as in other areas of life. Ariens are competitive by nature and even the quiet Arien enjoys the hunt. Prospective partners wearing their hearts on their sleeves may not hold the Arien interest for long. Ariens need partners who appreciate their strength and independence. The Arien male has a fierce instinctive pride to be the provider, a type of 'Me Tarzan, you Jane' approach. The Arien female is also self-sufficient; she can be a tower of strength and encouragement for her mate during hard times.

The Aries-Libra polarity

It is impossible to assess the Aries characteristics without taking into consideration the reflex action of the opposite sign of Libra. The Aries-Libra polarity is a guiding, maintaining influence. Whilst the kidneys (Libra) function to balance the water in the body and prevent a build-up of toxins, the brain (Aries) is the 'source' of conscious and subconscious activity of the bodily functions. If the brain is impaired, the most basic functions are modified and will cease to perform efficiently. The Aries-Libra polarity also maintains the acid/alkaline balance and the sodium/potassium balance in the body as well as the passive/aggressive balance within the psyche.

The wisdom of Aries

Aries is the first sign of the zodiac, the first cry, the start of life from which all future development stems and without which, there would be no future development.

Ariens must learn to be still, learn to be happy just 'to be' in order to relish the dynamic action of life. Before Ariens burn out, they must allocate time to top-priority items like self, loved ones, diet and health. They should practise moderation and contrast.

♉ TAURUS: 21 APRIL TO 20 MAY

The symbol of Taurus shows the head and horns of the bull, with the horns reaching upward to attract and conserve spiritual and material offerings from the universe. Taurus is a fixed Earth sign, denoting loyalty, dedication, and practicality. Few signs can match the generosity and protectiveness the Taurus person demonstrates towards those they love. The ability of Taurus to 'earth' high-flying ideals and inspirations frequently attracts to them people who seek reassurance and anchorage. The more obstacles to overcome, the harder the Taurus person will persevere to overcome them. Healthwise they do not bend or break easily, but when they are ill, they take longer to recover than many of the other zodiac signs.

Taureans usually have a highly developed sense of taste, touch and smell and as such, the Taurean appreciation of beauty knows no bounds. With regard to eating habits, some Taurean people can suffer as a result of eating too many rich foods, incompatible food combinations and too little of the right foods. Consequently the build-up of toxins in the body will lead to sluggishness and discomfort in the liver and gall regions. Love is a powerful Taurean motivating factor and it is common for persons born under Taurus to associate food with love. Taurus is the chef extraordinaire, the spoiler of loved ones.

The sign of Taurus governs the throat, tonsils, neck, jugulars and thyroid gland. If Taureans are run down, it quickly becomes apparent to them through the inflammation and tenderness felt in these areas.

Taurus is ruled by the planet Venus, which has an affinity with art and music. The Taurean association with the throat endows many Taureans with a rich-speaking or singing voice and a deep appreciation of the fine arts. Those born under the sign of Taurus should read the section on Venus cycles in Chapter 6, for the cycles and activation of Venus are of special significance to the lives of Taurean people.

Psychologically, of all the zodiac signs, Taurus is one of the most loved and admired for their sense of loyalty. Taureans make wonderful friends, especially for those who like to feel needed. If they have given up on someone, it will only be after they have exhausted all possible avenues to make the relationship work. But this very trait is a double-edged sword which can make it difficult for Taureans to recognise when to let go, even when they know the party is over. The inability to let go of the past can sometimes generate a sense of failure and the great Taurean challenge in life is to accept that which is given and that which is taken away.

The patient stubbornness of Taurus often gives them a streak of perfectionism; if channelled artistically, they can be brilliant at what they do. But the perfectionism can sometimes border on obsession. Over-compensating behaviour can stem from a deep need for security.

The sign of Taurus is about values and value judgments and whilst Taureans support certain values wholeheartedly, they may be inflexible about accepting others' values, especially the values of those in their spiritual care, such as their children.

In love, Taureans must have a great love in their lives. There is nothing half-hearted about Taurean lovers; their great affection, combined with an intensity bordering on obsession, can give them an enormous capacity to love. In many cases the love is sublimated into a love of God, art or humanity, but due to their earthiness, is usually expressed in a tangible way — through direct giving. If blocked or deprived, the love can be misdirected and express itself in unusual forms. In this instance the magnificent obsession loses its lustre.

Taurus is a sign of the senses — touch, smell, hearing and taste

— and Taureans need direct physical contact with others.

The Taurus-Scorpio polarity

Robert Carl Jansky in his book *Astrology, Nutrition and Health*, describes the Taurus-Scorpio polarity as the 'consumptive, eliminative and procreative' function. Foods are taken in through the mouth and down the throat, ruled by Taurus. Waste air is exhaled through the mouth, a Taurus function. Scorpio governs the reproductive system and the rectum. The wastes of the digestive process are excreted via Scorpio. It is common for the Taurus person to suffer from complaints of the reproductive system (Scorpio) and for Scorpio persons to suffer from the throat problems of Taurus.

The wisdom of Taurus

Taureans must learn to feel safe, so that they can enjoy the beauty of what they have created around them, without relying too much on external trappings. Obsessions can be beautiful and highly creative, but Taureans should be selective about their obsessions.

♊ GEMINI: 21 MAY TO 21 JUNE

The symbol of Gemini is the twins, the pairs found in Nature. An alternative symbol describes two pieces of wood bound together, symbolising contradictory mental processes. Gemini is a mutable Air sign, forever in motion, seeking an escape from boredom. Gemini has a marvellous capacity for abstract thinking; it is one of the great intellectual signs, so it is important for the Gemini to seek intellectual challenges. Unexpressed mental activity can create unnecessary worry and anxiety complexes.

Gemini is ruled by Mercury, the Messenger of the gods. Roman mythology describes Mercury as the God of Language and Geminis are masters of communication and literacy, clever and quick-witted. Many Geminis are writers and most are bookworms. They are the most comfortable in professions which require them to communicate and mix with others — the old cliché 'Busy minds are happy minds' must have been written for a Gemini. Geminis enjoy a changeable environment, or choose to be in continual motion themselves. There is a swiftness of action and a youthful demeanour, and many are endowed with a natural sense of rhythm and dance. Geminis have an affinity with young people, even when they are of the older generation. Those born under the sign of Gemini should also read the section on Mercury cycles in Chapter 6. The cycles and activation of Mercury are of special significance to the lives of Gemini people.

The body areas governed by Gemini are the hands, arms and shoulders. There is frequently a preoccupation with the hands through gesturing, knitting, handcrafts, writing or nail-biting, but many Geminis have beautiful and graceful hands. Gemini also governs the nervous systems; hands which are kept occupied can vent and level out nervous tensions. Gemini rules the lungs, diaphragm and tubes of the body. Good, clean air is essential to the well-being of Geminis, but many are attracted to smoking, which involves activity for the hands and lungs, plus a relaxant for the nervous system. As all these body areas are vulnerable Gemini points, Geminis are highly susceptible to the side-effects of smoking.

Psychologically, the duality of the sign of Gemini suggests many life-expressions. In some instances I have met Geminis in search of the big obsession, often in the autumn of their lives. But Geminis should not compare themselves to the zodiac signs who find it natural to focus on one point to the exclusion of all else. There are many high achievers in dual-focus areas of life, so it is important for Geminis to recognise the advantages of their duality, rather than believe they are missing out on some important life jewel.

Geminis are capable of great responsibility, but their psyche demands a sense of freedom; they like to have fun. Anyone trying to load a Gemini down with problems and responsibilities which the Gemini has not elected to shoulder, will soon observe the second dimension of Gemini.

Dissatisfaction and boredom can force Geminis into a vicious circle of hyperactivity, with little time for rest and meditation. As they are often 'of two minds' about certain issues, Geminis are prone to nervous exhaustion and must work to find peace within themselves.

In love, Geminis are frequently distracted, because it is hard for them to ignore a friendly smile. Because of their intense interest in people, they are often accused of being light-hearted about their relationships. But Geminis are capable of long-term, loving relationships provided the partner holds their interest, or they have another stimulating outlet for their physical and mental energies, such as a hobby, course of study or teaching activity.

The Gemini-Sagittarius polarity

This polarity represents interaction and movement, thought and mobility, abstract and philosophical concepts. There is some danger within this polarity of getting caught up in trivia and miscellaneous areas of life, so the thoughts should be strongly directed towards developing the higher faculties. The lungs and connecting tubes within the body (Gemini) move oxygen and nourishment. The hips and thighs of Sagittarius provide movement and grace to transport the body itself and assist in self-expression.

The wisdom of Gemini

Geminis like to socialise, mix and match, but should learn to be still within. They will find peace through ordered thinking, correct breathing and meditation.

♋ CANCER: 22 JUNE TO 22 JULY

The symbol of Cancer shows the folded claws of the crab, denoting the retentive, nurturing spirit of the sign. The symbol is also said to represent the female breasts. Like the crab, Cancerians can sometimes present crusty personalities to the world in order to protect their vulnerable interior. When hurt they react by withdrawing into their shells, physically and emotionally hiding from real and imagined traumas. Their protectiveness extends to those they love, and Cancerians will vehemently defend those in their care from unfavourable outside influences.

Cancer is a cardinal Water sign, sensitive but enterprising, preferring to lead than to be led. There is a wonderful sense of caring for others which can be expressed through nursing, catering, shopkeeping and on a larger scale, through public relations work. Keep in mind that the crab is a collector by nature. As a result, Cancerians retain what is received by them and nothing is lost. This can apply to memories, shells, photographs, stamps or money. Cancer is an excellent business sign, especially if the business is small and personalised.

Cancerians are sentimental; they love history and family trees. The most vulnerable factor in the life of the Cancerian is their family, which can include the parental home, their own marriage or their offspring. In some instances a Cancerian will have unrealistic expectations of the family and I have seen many withdraw from loved family members to avoid mental anguish. I have concluded that Cancerians need an exceptional input of love from their family during their formative years. If they are one of an average family where competition reigns, they often feel unloved. Cancerians should try to dispense with idealistic family illusions and think of their family members as people with human frailties.

There is also another type of Cancerian, often an only child, who has enjoyed royal treatment at home, but who could take a few years to adjust to the world outside the safety of the nest, due to a reluctance to modify certain ties.

Cancer is ruled by the Moon, signifying the subconscious mind; people born under the sign of Cancer should follow the monthly cycles of the Moon as their moods and emotions are prone to rapid fluctuation at certain periods in the cycle, in particular around the full Moon. Read Chapters 5 and 6 on the Moon cycles and lunar phases. The subconscious mind of the Cancerian is rich and fertile, so it is not surprising that the Moon and the sign of Cancer is prominent in the charts of many famous writers.

The body areas governed by Cancer are the stomach, breasts and membrane coverings of areas such as the brain and lungs. When Cancerians are upset they frequently suffer from stomach nerves, indigestion and eventually ulcers. To some extent the liver is also vulnerable. In times of stress Cancerians are strongly advised to adhere to a light, but highly nourishing, diet.

Psychologically, as a water sign governed by the Moon, Cancerians can be very emotional. It is important for them to confront their emotions and deal with them, otherwise they may end up laughing on the outside and crying on the inside. Mood swings can be unsettling to the Cancerian who often seeks ways to stabilise the inner tides. Like all the Water signs, Cancerians must be wary of props such as alcohol and tranquillisers. Personal contact with water in activities such as swimming and sailing, will have a calming effect.

In love, Cancerians are romantic, tender, vulnerable and sensuous. Most Cancerians have a genuine desire to establish a relationship based on love, make a home and become a parent. The happy home is the ultimate fulfilment for the Cancerian and those who are contented at home have the ability to reach unequalled heights in the outside world. The Cancerian will not respect a partner who does not share their own good business sense; the partner must contribute and provide some of the ideas and inspiration. Once the commitment has been made and the security established , however, the Cancerian will remain steadfast. Cancerians are known to remain in unsatisfactory relationships because of a reluctance to let go. Think of the crab in danger, which will attack and hold on until the end.

The Cancer-Capricorn polarity

Cancer is the defender, the protective casing for the body membranes. Capricorn is the bony structure, the knees, joints and skin. Cancer represents the absorption of food in the stomach, Capricorn the final result of the nutritional value of what is eaten. Incompatible foods will become visibly obvious as a skin complaint and physically obvious as calcification and pain in the joints.

The wisdom of Cancer

Cancerians must gather their strength and confront emotional traumas. They should recognise that family members are not gods or demi-gods. For the sake of their own happiness, they should accept and love their 'less-than-ideal' family.

♌ Leo: 23 July to 22 August

The symbol of Leo shows the tail or mane of the lion, representing the power and energy of the sign and all that is dignified, proud and warm.

Leo is a fixed Fire sign, ruled by the Sun, which is the centre of our solar system. Like the Sun, Leos generate a mystical radiation of magnetic vitality. In a room full of people it is the Leo who is usually found in the centre of a circle, surround by people who are basking in this invisible force. Read Chapter 6 on the solar return cycle: the cycles and activation of the Sun have considerable repercussion in the lives of Leos.

Leos like to think big and refuse to accept limitations; it is important for them to feel they are special. Because of their innate ability to encourage and inspire others, they make excellent managers and teachers. Leos are usually straightforward and dislike underhandedness. They make loyal and generous friends.

There is a dash of Professor Higgins in every Leo, who relishes the idea of taking someone under their wing and generally guiding them on their way, giving the Leo a sense of power and achievement.

Leos have a strongly competitive spirit, which frequently attracts them to competitive sport and politics. But the personal expectation of being number one places them under a lot of pressure to eliminate the competition — their pride can therefore hinder their progress.

The body areas governed by Leo are the heart, spine and back. Leos have exceptional recuperative powers but as a result of the heavy load of responsibility most Leos take upon themselves, they may also suffer from overstrain, overheating and fevers. It is essential for Leos to educate themselves at an early age as to the correct way to lift heavy objects, simply because I have rarely met a Leo who has not suffered from some form of back strain. In addition, Leos would be advised to become involved in a regular exercise programme to strengthen the back muscles and avoid a build-up of pressure in the chest. A regular massage would be a valuable addition to their routine.

Psychologically, there are two types of Leos — the strong, outgoing, dominating personality and the shy, tensioned sufferer. Neither type will go unnoticed. The healthiest environment for Leos is one where they are loved and appreciated; sometimes they forsake deeper relationships to achieve this state. The Leos who feel their sterling qualities are recognised will be generous to a fault. Leos thrive on enjoyment and whilst they work hard, the love to play. Emotionally there is a child-like quality about them, which makes them extremely gullible to flattery.

In love, affairs of the heart will play an important role in the lives of all Leos. Their spontaneity attracts a large proportion of Leos to an early love affair or marriage. Leos will not be dictated to in love, so they require a partner who appreciates their strength and will not be threatened by it. They make proud and protective parents, who are happy to share their time and show interest in their offspring.

The Leo-Aquarius polarity
Leo rules the heart, which pumps blood and energy through the body. Aquarius rules the circulation, which distributes the blood pumped by the heart (Leo). This polarity represents the generation and continuity of the life force.

The Wisdom of Leo
Leos should not be taken in by false flattery. They should distinguish between those who are true and those who are false and thus fulfil their objective of loyal friendships. Leos should pursue a creative outlet so as not to waste their power and talent.

♍ VIRGO: 23 AUGUST TO 22 SEPTEMBER
The symbol of Virgo shows a maiden holding a green branch, an ear of corn or a spike of grain in her hand. This is symbolic of the fertility of crops as Virgo is an Earth sign and a child of Nature. Virgo represents the work and service required to product the crops.

Virgo strives for moral purity, expressed in a quest for perfectionism. Virgos analyse and dissect the whole in order to digest the truth, but unfortunately this trait is often misinterpreted by others as over-criticism. However, Virgos are usually severe judges of themselves as well as others and excel in careers where good powers of observation and a keen attention to detail is required. They make excellent accountants, nurses, craftspersons, watchmakers and secretaries. Virgo is strongly represented in the horoscopes of classical musicians where precision, timing and accuracy is paramount. I have personally noticed the sign of Virgo strongly represented in the fashion industry, which is associated with shapes, form and detail.

As a mutable Earth sign, Virgo has an affinity with Nature and plants. Even flat-dwelling Virgos usually have lush herb gardens to brighten up their environment. An important aspect to the sign of Virgo is their natural awareness of correct diet and cooking procedures, which they may or may not adhere to. But as a result, Virgos make excellent advisers on natural remedies, homoeopathic treatments, preventative medicines and manipulative forms of healing.

The body areas governed by Virgo are the intestinal tract, the duodenum, the spleen and co-rulership of the liver. As such, Virgos must be discriminating about the foods they eat otherwise they will be susceptible to colitis, diarrhoea, constipation and other intestinal disorders. Some Virgos find that they cannot easily absorb heavy foods such as meat, especially after the age of forty. It is important for Virgos to experiment with their diets to establish which foods and substances agree with them and eliminate those which are disrupting their bodily functions.

Virgo is ruled by Mercury, the planet of logic, abstract thought and nervous energy. Mercury operates in a more practical and physical manner ruling Virgo than it does the Air sign Gemini, which it co-rules. Consequently, in its Virgo mode, the ideas and thought patterns of Mercury operate through the physical body, the environment and material security. Virgos are susceptible to physical illness as a result of nervous strain. Natural worriers, they often suffer from psychosomatic disorders, although the security-consciousness of their Earth element guarantees that there will be plenty of precautionary measures in the form of natural remedies and cures in the home. Read the section on the Mercury cycle in Chapter 6; the cycles and activation of Mercury have considerable repercussion in the lives of Virgos.

Psychologically, the quest for purity, which is so deeply ingrained in the Virgo psyche, makes it difficult for them to accept compromise. A high level of mental energy makes complete relaxation a challenge, especially if repetitive worry cycles display obsessional overtones. Such an overload of complex mental energy can generate negativity. Yoga combines the mental and physical disciplines and helps to sublimate and dissipate the negativity.

In love, although Virgos can be cool and independent, their love burns with a white heat. They will forsake all to be with the loved one, who is sometimes accredited with non-existent qualities, as it is not uncommon for idealistic Virgos to project the perfect image onto their lovers. If the relationship fails the Virgo will frequently carry the love within his or her heart, because Virgo is not a sign of compromise. Virgos do not seek a partner for the sake of partnership and they may refuse to replace their ideal love with another, less perfect match. It is important for Virgos to select partners who will broaden their horizons as they can get caught up with details, often to the exclusion of major issues. Virgos need space to broaden their intellectual horizons and they are happiest with small families and flexibility to develop what they often term their 'child of the mind'.

The Virgo-Pisces polarity
This polarity is related to defence, resistance and discrimination. Virgo governs the intestinal tract, spleen and liver and Pisces the lymph glands and feet. Virgo-Pisces confronts disease and poisons ingested in the body, and deals with the toxic invaders. Modern society has created an overload of toxicity in the environment, so there is an increase of allergy-related conditions. Those in the Virgo-Pisces polarity have a responsibility to themselves to take additional preventative measures. Moderation in all things is their only road to health and happiness.

The Wisdom of Virgo
By loving themselves and others, Virgos will learn to accept a few mistakes in themselves and other people. They should quieten their mental pace. If they concentrate too much on the trees, they may lose sight of the forest.

♎ LIBRA: 23 SEPTEMBER TO 22 OCTOBER
The symbol of Libra shows a set of scales, representing balance and justice. Libra is a cardinal Air sign; the double line of power in the symbol of Libra is consistent with the enterprise and intellect associated with the sign.

Librans have a tendency to weigh up life. In order to deal with a discrepancy of justice, they must weigh up both sides of a situation as they perceive it. Although Librans strive for peace and harmony, they will harbour repressed hostility if justice is denied. They prefer the line of least resistance and dislike confrontation — and yet somehow attract it. It is not surprising therefore to find the sign of Libra strongly represented in the horoscopes of army generals and sporting figures.

Librans make good lawyers, marriage and human rights counsellors, managers and technologists. Venus, the planet of love, art and beauty, is the ruler of Libra, and the co-ruler of Taurus. Librans are frequently labelled the 'beautiful people' of the zodiac. Many are attracted to careers in art, music, design and the beauty industry, as they perceive the human form as the ultimate objet d'art. Read the section on Venus cycles in Chapter 6, for the cycles and activation of Venus have considerable repercussion in the lives of Librans.

As an air sign, Libra is a communicator and a diplomat. To say that relationships are important to Librans is a gross understatement. Librans thrive mentally, physically and spiritually through a happy and harmonious balance with others. If the scales become upset or unbalanced, or a personal relationship goes wrong, they can become frustrated, tense and sometimes physically ill.

The body areas governed by Libra are the kidneys, adrenal glands and acid-alkaline balance. As the efficient filtering and regulating action of the kidneys is essential to life, Librans must keep their kidneys flushed out with plenty of fresh water, otherwise they could be prone to cystitis, kidney stones, kidney infection and inflammations. Discrimination is required regarding an excessive intake of sweets and high-acid foods such as meat. Lack of attention to personal health can make some Librans susceptible to diabetes and Bright's disease.

Psychologically, the Libran weighing-up process can lead to indecision. By the time both sides of the question are seriously considered, a good opportunity could pass. Love is an important motivating factor for Librans. Libran love is thoughtful love, a determination of love through the use of the thought processes, a great love of the thought processes and mental awareness of the power of their own ability to love and be loved.

In love, Librans are charming and romantic. They have rich experiences in love and frequently fall in love with love itself. Librans will search until they find the 'other half'. Although the physical side of the relationship is important, the partner will need to share the Libran cultural and intellectual interests. Librans are happiest in subdued surroundings with balanced colour schemes and their favourite music.

The Libra-Aries polarity

The Libran-Aries polarity maintains the passive/aggressive balance with the psyche, the acid/alkaline balance and the sodium/potassium balance. Aries, the Fire sign is able to burn up and absorb heavy foods more efficiently than Libra, the Air sign. To assist the guiding, maintaining influence of this polarity, Librans should adhere to sensible dietary principles. The kidneys (Libra) balance the water in the body and help prevent a build-up of toxins. The brain (Aries) is the source of conscious and subconscious activity of the bodily functions.

The wisdom of Libra

Inner beauty and harmony are equally as important as external appearances. Indecision can lower self-confidence, so Librans should take a stand.

♏ SCORPIO: 23 OCTOBER TO 22 NOVEMBER

The sign of Scorpio is frequently given dual symbolism — that of the eagle and the scorpion. The eagle is a bird of great power and wonder, capable of taking flight and rising high above Earthly considerations and temptations. The more commonly accepted symbol depicts the legs and tail of the scorpion, a feared creature with a deadly sting. In ancient times the sign of Scorpio was cursed as being evil and associated with the serpent in the Garden of Eden, symbolising man's choice to rule, or be ruled, by the sexual act.

Scorpio is a fixed Water sign, signifying determination, passion, intuition and unequalled emotional intensity. It is ruled by Pluto, the planet of power, birth and rebirth, death, obsession, sainthood and the underworld. If you are a Scorpio, take special note of the section on Pluto cycles in Chapter 9; the activation of Pluto has considerable repercussion in the lives of Scorpios.

When considering the extremity of interpretation attributed to Pluto, it is not surprising that Scorpio is the sign which is the most extreme in its expression. If the power behind the Scorpio personality is directed towards the betterment of humanity, the results will be extraordinary and the person exceptional, but if the power is directed with equal intensity towards the lower side of human nature, the downhill path is taken with equal fervour.

Many believe that there are two types of Scorpios, but it is more likely that there are Scorpios at different stages of development. Scorpios in their highest form have a desire to penetrate the material with the spiritual. Others direct much of their passion into creativity, intellectual achievements and inspired activity. Unfortunately there are also the self-destructive Scorpios who squander their available reserves of energy and feel compelled to exploit themselves.

The body areas governed by Scorpio are the reproductive system, colon, prostrate gland, bladder and immune system. Scorpios are secretive and tend to hide their intense emotions, which requires a large measure of discipline. This act of 'holding on' can make them especially prone to constipation or other disorders of the excretory system. Scorpios must learn to let go, otherwise the build-up of toxins in their body will affect their attitude towards those around them. Natural cleansing remedies will improve their physical and mental well-being.

Psychologically, Scorpios are direct and have no half-baked ideas; their feelings are black and white. They have a compulsive urge to fulfil their potential, which is usually accompanied by sacrifice, either for themselves or for those who love them. If they do not give themselves licence to follow their true path in life, they can be self-destructive, because deep within the Scorpio there is a rejection of mediocrity.

Scorpios are powerful. An excess of power can be enlightening or destructive for those in possession of it. When Scorpios are 'at war' with themselves, it is difficult for them to recognise and acknowledge a problem. And when the problem is finally resolved, they may find it hard to leave the past behind them.

In love, Scorpios are intense. They are often surprised by the effect they have on others. When they give, the quality of their giving is extraordinary. Scorpios demand complete fidelity from their lovers, so sensitive souls take heed — think twice before you get in over your head, or you may be the goldfish in the piranha bowl. Scorpios are possessive lovers. But the Scorpio with a mission in life will sublimate the passion and may join a religious order.

The Scorpio-Taurus polarity

This polarity relates to the extremities of the nutritional process through the link between the mouth and throat (Taurus) and the organs of excretion (Scorpio). Human life is sustained through the intake of food (Taurus), to be processed. The cycle ends with the excretion of waste (Scorpio). The cycle then begins again with the next meal. The Scorpio-Taurus polarity therefore relates to birth, death and rebirth. The reproductive cycle is also linked to the polarity.

The wisdom of Scorpio

By letting go, Scorpios will cleanse their bodies and souls. They should forgive and forget.

♐ SAGITTARIUS: 23 NOVEMBER TO 21 DECEMBER

The symbol of Sagittarius depicts an arrow and section of a bow. A centaur, or half-man, half-horse figure who holds the bow and arrow, represents the conflict between man's philosophical mind and the carnal instinct of conquest. The arrows of truth aim for the heavens, but when the truth penetrates, the arrows can be sharp. People born under the sign of Sagittarius are well-known for their frankness and love of truth.

Sagittarius is a mutable Fire sign, with all the drive, enthusiasm, ambition and energy of Aries and Leo, the other two fire signs, but with added mobility and flexibility. Sagittarius is ruled by Jupiter, the planet of faith, optimism and expansion on all levels. The Sagittarian needs are many: most Sagittarians desire to improve their education, expand their philosophical horizons, attain recognition and success, and enjoy a comfortable existence and happy personal life. They want it all and usually have what it takes to get it. If you are a Sagittarian, take special note of the section on Jupiter cycles in Chapter 7. The activation of Jupiter has considerable repercussion in the lives of Sagittarians.

The sign of Sagittarius and its ruler Jupiter, are associated with both sides of the law, moral issues, politics, insurance, printing, publishing, promotions, business in general and travel; many Sagittarians establish successful careers in these areas. They have the ability to visualise the scope for large undertakings and most are not afraid to take a chance. Sagittarians are 'now' people, who become bored with routine and petty details. To be truly fulfilled, the Sagittarian must cover distance. As a result, few Sagittarians do not travel extensively in their lifetime. Sagittarians have a good sense of humour and an urge for freedom; consequently, they dislike people who behave like clinging vines.

The body areas governed by Sagittarius are the hips, thighs, sciatic nerve and liver. The high energy potential of the sign can attract Sagittarians to challenging sports and activities. As a result they are prone to strain and injury to the hips, thighs, sacrum and coccyx bone. Older Sagittarians frequently suffer from rheumatism in these areas. Sagittarians are attracted to rich living and gout and obesity could also become health problems unless moderation is exercised. The recuperative powers of Sagittarius are extremely good, however, provided they partake of some form of physical activity.

Psychologically, Sagittarians have wide horizons. They are optimistic and adventurous, so it is difficult for them to accept limitations and boundaries. To be placed in an environment where there is material or spiritual poverty could lead to illness — the Sagittarian must expand. Sagittarius is a moralising sign; consequently, Sagittarians have a responsibility to work together with others in the application of their ethics, as some can be a law unto themselves.

In love, Sagittarians will be as warm and wonderful as they are in other areas, but will need to express their freedom-loving natures through work or interests, otherwise they could become bored and restless. In any relationship Sagittarians will place a high value on retaining their own individuality. Sagittarians make good partners but they prefer marriage and parenthood to fit into their lifestyle, rather than having to conform to a standard mould. The sign of Sagittarius has an affinity with multi-cultures — many Sagittarians form lasting partnerships with people from entirely different backgrounds to their own.

The Sagittarian-Gemini polarity

This polarity represents interaction and movement, thought and mobility, abstract and philosophical thought. The lungs and connecting tubes within the body (Gemini) move oxygen and nourishment. The hips and thighs of Sagittarius provide movement and grace to transport the body itself and assist in self-expression. In her book *The American Book of Nutrition and Medical Astrology,* Eileen Nauman lists exhaled breath under Sagittarius. She states: —

> *'Whereas Sagittarius represents exhaled breath, Gemini represents inhaled breath. This oxygenation that reaches the blood is of utmost concern: without proper amounts of oxygen, a person will feel mentally dull and tired.'*

The wisdom of Sagittarius

Sagittarians should aim for the highest star and live to enjoy their expansive spirit, but should acknowledge realistic boundaries and respect the right of others to formulate their own boundaries.

♑ CAPRICORN: 22 DECEMBER TO 20 JANUARY

The sign of Capricorn was considered by the ancients to be the most important of all the zodiac signs. The symbol of Capricorn shows the goat climbing steadily on an upward path in life. An alternative symbol shows a goat with a curling fish tail, called Capricornus by the Chaldeans, and associated with the mythical 'Culture Gods', who came from the sea to teach humans the ways of civilisation.

Capricorn is a cardinal Earth sign with great inner drive, which is expressed in a practical manner. Capricorn is ruled by Saturn, the planet of responsibility, wisdom and limitation. As a rule, Capricorns display a gradual unfoldment of their potential; their lives gaining rapid momentum after the first Saturn return at the age of 29 years. They have not been static before then, but somehow Capricorns gain new insight and confidence as they approach the age of thirty. Often they experience hard times in their childhood, either through personal shyness and inhibitions, difficult circumstances in the home, a family health problem or a separation. If you are a Capricorn, take special note of the section on Saturn cycles in Chapter 7 for the activation of Saturn has considerable repercussion in the lives of Capricorns.

To the Capricorn, personal prestige, career prospects, education, breeding and background are important. Capricorns are dignified cautious and economical. They have an in-built respect for work, which enables them to achieve their ambitions through sheer perseverance. Capricorns have an affinity with the land, farming and Nature and during depressed times, can find joy in the outdoors.

As the polarity sign of Cancer, Capricorn is the other family-orientated sign. Capricorns approach their families as the protectors and providers. It is they who take responsibility for the 'black sheep' of the family and the ageing relatives, giving moral and financial support where necessary. To the Capricorn, 'blood runs thicker than water'. Many astrologers believe that Capricorns have 'old souls'; they have a special communication with elderly people and even the Capricorn children have a wisdom beyond their years. Perhaps Capricorns respect the dignity and wealth of experience which accompanies old age. It is not unusual for a Capricorn child to be born to older parents. In later years when the mother is experiencing menopause, the Capricorn child may be commencing puberty — a type of 'beginning and ending' cycle within that family.

The body areas governed by Capricorn are the knees, joints, bones, skin, hair, teeth, nails and gall bladder. Capricorns are prone to chills, stiffness and calcification. It is important for them to practise physical and mental flexibility — massage will aid relaxation and circulation. Lubrication, through the intake of adequate fluids and the correct natural oils, will keep the body supple and the skin clear.

Psychologically, Capricorns are reserved and tend to emotionally distance themselves from others, which can be effective in business, but which can create barriers in intimate relationships. They need partners who are sensitive and expressive; partners who will perceive their inner warmth and help them to overcome their shyness. Capricorns have deep feelings which need expression and they can become very depressed in their isolation. I have noticed a wonderful dry wit and a natural sense of timing in the Capricorn personality. Their discipline and practical creativity attracts many to the theatre, either as performers, organisers or spectators. All Capricorns should endeavour to cultivate their creative potential and in this area, rise above Earth-bound considerations.

In love, Capricorns are cautious, modest and selective. Marriage to a Capricorn is not a fairytale affair — it is a serious step in life, only to be taken after thought and preparation. Love is important to the Capricorn, but sharing and pursuing life's goals is a pre-requisite. The words of Antoine De Saint-Exupery could almost be a Capricorn philosophy:–

'Love does not consist in gazing at each other but in looking together in the same direction.'

Capricorns are often attracted to relationships involving an appreciable age difference between the partners. They may not be effervescent in their passion, but they are loving and loyal. Like good wine, Capricorn relationships improve with time. Children are sacred in the Capricorn family and so are the old-fashioned rules such as respect, manners and self-discipline. Capricorns express their love by providing physical and emotional security for their family.

The Capricorn-Cancer polarity

Cancer represents the absorption of food in the stomach, Capricorn the final result of the nutritional value of what is eaten. Incompatible foods will become visibly obvious as a skin complaint or through hair which lacks lustre. They will become physically obvious as calcification, pain in the joints, toothache, inflammation of the gall bladder, or worse still, gall stones. Capricorns should seek guidance from their naturopaths concerning diets to suit their specific requirements, and should pay special attention to correct mineral requirements.

The wisdom of Capricorn

Excessive denial of personal creativity can lead to depression and frugality of thought. Others will be more responsive if the Capricorn learns more self-love. Capricorns should give themselves licence to work less and enjoy life more.

♒ AQUARIUS: 21 JANUARY TO 19 FEBRUARY

The symbol of Aquarius shows a water-bearer pouring the contents from his urn to quench the thirst of humanity. The glyph resembles the graphic representation of electro-magnetic waves. The waves of water are symbolic of intuition and inspiration. In modern times the waves are said to represent waves of electricity and light.

Aquarius is a fixed Air sign, denoting intelligence beyond reason, an independent viewpoint, magnetic power and stubborness. Aquarians have a deep concern for humanity, an all-embracing universal love, the desire for the establishment of equal human rights and deep feelings of friendship towards fellow creatures.

Aquarius is the most unusual sign of the zodiac. Because of their futuristic thinking, Aquarians are often regarded as eccentric and unconventional. Aquarius is ruled by Uranus, the planet of radical action, revolution and sudden reform, which is a direct contrast to the fixed quality of the sign. The Uranian influence can generate occasional abrupt and unusual changes in the lives of Aquarians, especially at specific periods during the Uranus cycle (see Chapter 8, 'Uranus Cycles and your Health').

The intellectual nature of the sign, combined with a natural understanding of human nature, attracts many Aquarians to careers in psychological analysis, councelling and welfare work. Aquarians like to spread the word, so many are found working in advertising, the media and as writers or teachers. The Aquarian inventiveness is often linked to brilliant scientific discoveries and technological research.

The body areas governed by Aquarius are the calves, ankles and blood circulation. An exercise programme to improve and regulate the muscle coordination will maintain a healthy circulation and help prevent leg cramps and varicose veins. Aquarians can sometimes be absent-minded; a lack of oxygen can produce vagueness, so a sound exercise programme has the added advantage of assisting the oxygenation of the body.

Psychologically, Aquarians are loyal and trusting people who are not easily swayed once their mind is made up. Despite their futuristic thinking, they, like all the fixed signs, find it hard to mentally release something which has hurt or worried them.

Aquarians like to sell an idea to others, but will not buy an idea themselves without time to analyse and formulate its worth. They will find irresistible anything which is unusual, innovative and has a touch of magic or science-fiction to it.

In love, Aquarians dislike feeling tied down. They are frequently eye-catching and trendy in appearance. They usually require time out to pursue friendships, clubs, societies and studies, which is where they tend to meet their partners. Aquarians are romantic and enjoy fantasising about their love interests. The Aquarian relationship invariably commences as a friendship, which blossoms into a friendship of lovers. If the friendship dies, so too does the romance. Aquarians like people and tend to attract them. They relate well to both sexes on a purely platonic level but jealous partners may not understand this trait.

The Aquarius-Leo polarity
Leo rules the heart, which pumps blood and energy through the body. Aquarius rules the circulation, which distributes the blood pumped by the heart (Leo). This polarity represents the generation and continuity of the life force. The high mental vibration of Aquarius requires maximum oxygenation to maintain the brain function at its peak.

The Wisdom of Aquarius
It is not necessary for Aquarians to renounce personal love in favour of impersonal multi-contacts and humanitarian pursuits. The thoughts of Aquarians will be captured by great projects, events from the past and plans for the future — they should anchor a part of themselves to the present.

♓ PISCES: 20 FEBRUARY TO 20 MARCH
The symbol of Pisces shows two fish swimming in opposite directions. It represents two sides of a person — the material and spiritual, and the conflicting expansive and restrictive elements within the self. It is the struggle of the soul within the body. Early Egyptian symbols depict Pisces as two fish swimming in the same direction. In these modern times the material and spiritual factors are being forced further apart — perhaps this is depicted in the modern symbol of Pisces.

Pisces is a mutable Water sign, shimmering, fluid-like, sensitive and inspirational. It is ruled by Neptune, the planet of intangible reality. If you were born under the sign of Pisces, take special note of the section on Neptune cycles in Chapter 9. The activation of Neptune has important repercussions in the lives of Pisceans.

Pisceans are shaped by their prevailing circumstances, for they are the chameleons of the zodiac, taking on the colours of their environment. Pisceans often adopt the characteristics of those they admire, which is why they are frequently mistaken for other zodiac signs. This marked impressionability makes Pisceans natural impersonators, but indicates that they must be discriminating when selecting their friends and associates. Pisces can be a leaf, drifting with the tide, hoping that it will take them into calm waters; the key to their success is therefore the development of self-confidence.

Many Pisceans are psychic. They are usually in touch with their subconscious minds and the collective consciousness of humanity; these states give them faith in the unknown and a knowledge of what is, was and will be. As a result they can be found working in religious orders or in the areas of mysticism and psychological analysis.

Pisceans also work well in artistic professions such as music, dance, acting, painting and writing. Alternatively they are attracted to areas which involve service to others and which call upon their good listening skills; they therefore excel in careers such as nursing, counselling, secretarial or social work.

The body areas governed by Pisces are the feet and the lymph glands. Pisceans are not renowned for their strong constitutions and tend to drain their physical and emotional energy reserves easily. They are well advised to take regular rest days to restore their inner resources and explore the benefits available from foot massage and reflexology.

Pisceans are prone to emotional disorders and physical illnesses of a nervous origin. They have a sensitivity to medicines, drugs and alcohol and care should be taken to avoid over-indulgence, which will lead to water retention, reaction symptoms, chemical imbalance in the body and a state of dependency.

Psychologically, Pisceans frequently dislike the realities of life and either withdraw from them or over-compensate in another area. They have a deep understanding of others' suffering because they are usually victims themselves at some stage. It is important for Pisceans to mentally take themselves out of the victim class, by discarding self-pity and re-evaluating their own worth. It is not without reason that astrologers have labelled Pisces 'the garbage bin of the zodiac'. Other signs dump their rubbish into the Pisces space and it is easy for the Piscean to become a self-sacrificing martyr. Don't blame the other signs Pisces — you accepted the rubbish!

In love, Pisceans are sentimental, dreamy, considerate and impractical. They are attracted to dynamic partners who will help instil strength and confidence in them. The Neptune influence of the sign means that Pisceans are easily misinterpreted, so it is vital for them to make others fully aware of their perspectives and intentions. Pisceans often find themselves in awkward romantic situations, through the intervention of a third party, misunderstandings or religious conflicts. Pisceans are happiest when they are in love and involved in a secure partnership — they are a tower of strength for their loved ones.

The Pisces-Virgo polarity

This polarity is related to defence, resistance and discrimination. Virgo governs the intestinal tract, spleen and liver and Pisces the lymph glands and feet. The Virgo-Pisces polarity confronts disease and poisons ingested in the body and deals with the toxic invaders. Modern society has created an overload of toxicity in the environment, so that there is an increase in allergy-related conditions. Those in the Virgo-Pisces polarity have a responsibility to themselves to take additional preventive measures. Attention to the quality of the blood is paramount. Moderation in all things is the only road to health and happiness.

The wisdom of Pisces

Pisceans should strengthen their inner resources. Fear and negative emotions will encourage escapism. They should revel in their sensitivity, and not mistake it for weakness. There is plenty of scope to admire others, but Pisceans should take control of their own lives.

Chapter Four

Common Factors in Groups of Zodiac Signs — The Qualities and Elements

The zodiac signs are categorised into groups known as 'qualities' and 'elements' (or 'triplicities'). Each of the two groups will link your sign with others. Because of these common links it is important to consider your qualities group as a whole and your elements group as a whole. Such categorisation will enable you to fully understand the possible reflex action and causative factors of your personal health configuration.

As a rule the astrologer has twelve planets and points in the birth horoscope to categorise into qualities and elements. These categories assist the astrologer in assessing the strengths and weaknesses in the life of the individual. With only the Sun sign to consider, readers must make allowance for the fact that there will be additional factors which can apply. But as the centre of our solar system, the Sun is a major factor in the horoscope and its placement makes an important statement about our health and vitality.

THE QUALITIES

The qualities describe *how* you approach your life. They consist of three groups of four zodiac signs:

The cardinal signs — Aries, Cancer, Libra and Capricorn
The fixed signs — Taurus, Leo, Scorpio and Aquarius
The mutable signs — Gemini, Virgo, Sagittarius and Pisces

Whichever quality your Sun sign belongs to, consider the body areas of the other three signs in your group as a potential reflex polarity, demonstrating underlying causative factors for health conditions.

The cardinal signs

The common factor of Aries, Cancer, Libra and Capricorn is their enterprise and ambition. If ill, they will be interested in quickly getting to the cause of the complaint, which they regard as a hindrance, eradicating it and getting on with their lives.

THE CARDINAL CROSS

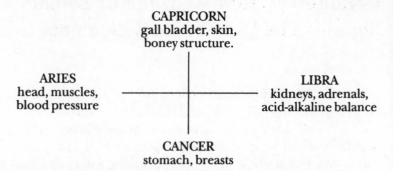

For example, the headaches attributed to Aries, can be linked to an upset stomach (Cancer) or a kidney disorder (Libra). Alternatively, unbalanced acid-alkaline levels (Libra) can manifest in the joints as stiffness or on the skin as blemishes (Capricorn).

The fixed signs

As a group, the fixed signs of Taurus, Leo, Scorpio and Aquarius are the most inflexible in the zodiac — loyal, dedicated, but highly resistant to change, unless of course they initiate the change. They are the ones most likely to 'soldier on' and deny their illness, despite the throbbing temples and raging fever. But when they finally succumb to illness, it is often quite serious and the healing process takes longer than the other qualities. Fixed signs can suffer from a systematic sluggishness and build-up of toxins, so that a good natural diet with plenty of roughage is essential to maintain their immunity to disease.

THE FIXED CROSS

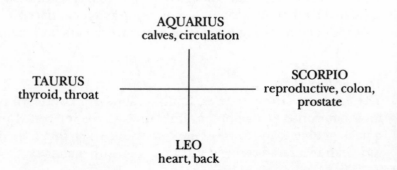

For example, the heart condition (Leo) or colon disorders (Scorpio) could well be attributed to a stubborn adherence to an old-fashioned diet of the same old foods, without acknowledgement of the body's changing needs. A build-up of toxins will be circulated (Aquarius) through the body and gradually undermine its defences.

Fixed signs often ignore biological and climatic changes, so they would be wise to consider a diet high in liquids, juices, fruit and vegetables and low in heavy meat dishes, for at least one or two days a week, in order to give their bodies the chance to bounce back and 'keep up' its good work. Look and listen to your body's needs. Move with the times.

The mutable signs

As a group, the mutable signs are flexible, adaptable and variable by nature. They are quick to become ill but with the right treatment, can make a rapid recovery. Their high output of nervous energy often results in fluctuating physical and mental vitality.

Mutable signs become bored unless the results of a new diet or treatment are instantaneous, and move on to new fads and therapists. Beware of mixing and matching your remedies and 'playing the home practitioner'. Reading a couple of textbooks does not make you the expert.

THE MUTABLE CROSS

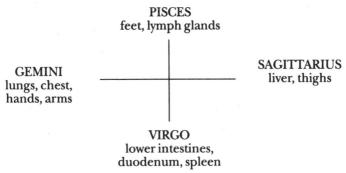

PISCES
feet, lymph glands

GEMINI
lungs, chest,
hands, arms

SAGITTARIUS
liver, thighs

VIRGO
lower intestines,
duodenum, spleen

Unless interest is shown in a healthy diet and lifestyle to nurture the defence system, the mutable signs will be susceptible to flu and other assorted viruses. They must be selective about their intake of alcohol, for what may be disguised as an illness could in fact be an allergy reaction. At some time in life, the sugar balance may need to be examined and regulated.

This is a sensitive group. Nervous anxiety and over-reaction can lead to illnesses with causes which are difficult to pinpoint.

The elements

The four elements of Fire, Earth, Air and Water have been represented in art, music and religion since the earliest recorded history of the human race, and form part of our heritage. The Greek philosopher Aristotle (384–322 BC) described the elements as follows: –

Fire as a combination of warmth and dryness

Earth as a combination of coldness and dryness

Air as a combination of warmth and moisture

Water as a combination of coldness and moisture

The Greeks associated the four elements with the signs of the zodiac:

Fire — the moral conduct, aspiration and spirit was associated with Aries, Leo and Sagittarius.

Earth — the body, its physical functions and requirements were associated with Taurus, Virgo and Capricorn.

Air — the mind and intellect were associated with Gemini, Libra and Aquarius.

Water — the emotions, soul yearnings and aestheticism were associated with Cancer, Scorpio and Pisces.

The zodiac signs of each element share a common factor, that of motivation. Therefore the elements which predominate at the moment of our birth indicate what motivates us. Even without a comprehensive knowledge of astrology, the reader can gain some understanding of his or her birth horoscope by studying the interpretation of the dominant element or elements. Those without a complete birth chart can concentrate on the element of their Sun sign.

Fire signs are motivated by energy and creativity.

Earth signs are motivated by perseverance and structured progress.

Air signs are motivated by intellect and the desire to communicate.

Water signs are motivated by instinct and emotion.

The Fire signs (Aries, Leo and Sagittarius)
The Fire signs are associated with action and pure energy, burning of the fuel and energy, the life force, a great appetite for life, sexual fire, instant combustion.

Positively expressed, Fire people will generate heat, enthusiasm, encouragement and movement. They usually have good digestive systems and excellent recuperative powers.

Negatively expressed, they can suffer from fevers, inflammations, acidity and illness or injury resulting from over-exertion, such as sudden haemorrhages, strains and accidents. Fire people who do not discover the correct level of self-expression of their powers become tense and suffer from an angry type of depression, often directed inwardly.

As an element, Fire can be a law unto itself, unrestrainable and overpowering, but when restrained, it can warm and light up the planet.

The Earth signs (Taurus, Virgo and Capricorn)
The Earth signs are associated with grounding, materialising, earthing dreams and ideals, spirituality made tangible, perseverance, ordered structure, discipline, the soil, crops and nutrition, conserving, discriminating, sensing.

Like the Earth itself, there is a solidarity and physical security about these people. Good health relates to good nutrition and many Earth people have a natural instinct as to which foods are right or wrong for them

Earth is affiliated with the digestive tract and is more likely than the other elements to retain some of the impurities from the foods they eat. Their sense of discrimination must therefore include their diet. Sluggish digestion can leave an accumulation of waste clogging up the system. Plenty of natural, non-toxic, cleansing foods and pure water will ensure efficient functioning.

The Air signs (Gemini, Libra and Aquarius)
The Air signs are associated with prana, breathing, the nervous and circulatory systems, communication, fraternising, balancing, thought, theory, ideas, logic, objectivity. — Air is all around us — nothing is hidden.

Air people can express themselves well, socialise and bring

people together with ease and charm. They are good helpers and advisers because it is possible for them to become involved in an objective manner. But if called upon to deal with the demands and emotions of others, many will endeavour to distance themselves in order to retain their buoyancy and sense of freedom, as they do not feel comfortable in a 'heavy' atmosphere. Air people suffer from lung complaints, nervous conditions and an over-active mind which can lead to insomnia and exhaustion. Many complain of wind in the digestive tract, which is often the direct result of gulping air and talking while eating.

The Water signs (Cancer, Scorpio and Pisces)

Water is the great mystifier, the element which can be readily converted by the other elements. It can be heated by fire and float into the air as steam. It can be frozen into a solid mass and absorbed by the earth. Time and heartache are the teachers from which Water signs will learn to take on their own shape and avoid negative influences.

Water has a natural urge to unify, become one with and empathise, so that objectivity is often difficult to achieve, even when it is required. But this quality can be a great asset in the caretaking professions such as counselling and nursing, when the suffering patient demands complete understanding.

Water is psychic, emotional and intuitive. Water is intangible, so that water people often seek out those with clearly defined personalities as partners and friends.

Negatively their sensitivity can lead them to stimulants such as alcohol and drugs, which dull the sensitivity, a sensitivity they perceive as physical or emotional pain. Water is secretive and seeks a safe harbour.

Water people suffer from emotional disorders, mucus discharges, colds, tumours and an incorrect water balance in the body. They are usually attracted to water itself, so should drink plenty of purified water, pamper themselves with oil baths and spend time in, on or near water.

MIXING AND MATCHING WITH OTHER ELEMENTS

With only your Sun sign at your disposal, you can compare the element of your sign with the elements of your family and friends. Remember that the Fire signs are Aries, Leo and Sagittarius; the Earth signs are Taurus, Virgo and Capricorn; the Air signs are Gemini, Libra and Aquarius and the Water signs are Cancer, Scorpio and Pisces.

FIRE AND AIR
Fire is highly compatible with Air, in that one feeds the other, creating a stimulating and volatile combination, usually accompanied by plenty of 'hot air'.

FIRE AND EARTH
Fire and Earth act like a volcano — powerful when active, semi-lethargic when inactive. This combination has strong potential for successful joint ventures.

FIRE AND WATER
Fire and Water is a steamy combination with alternating expressions of extremely hot or predominantly cool. A variable relationship for those who enjoy variety.

EARTH AND AIR
Earth and Air can generate a dust storm, which can obscure the direction of the relationship. However, it is a good combination which has the capacity to generate inventive ideas and apply them in a practical manner.

EARTH AND WATER
Earth and Water is one of the classic combinations with a high compatibility factor. A natural blending of elements which is fertile and productive. An imbalance of Earth and Water can also make mud and this combination has the potential to get 'bogged down'.

AIR AND WATER
Air and Water together will make plenty of froth and aerated bubbles. This can be an artistic match with alternating phases of sensitivity and sound commonsense.

TOO MUCH OR TOO LITTLE OF ONE ELEMENT

Medical astrologers have always maintained that the balance or imbalance of the elements in the birth horoscope plays a vital role in health diagnosis and preventative care. When the twelve planets and points of the birth horoscope are available to categorise into Fire, Earth, Air and Water, the reader is in a better position to interpret this section. Much has been written about an excess or lack of a particular element in the birth chart, but I have noticed some contradictory findings.

Most people have planets and points distributed over the four elements, but some have few in one particular element and an overload in another. It seems that those with a gap or an overload in their chart will make their presence felt, either for their sterling qualities or their notoriety.

The missing link will act as a magnet, often outweighing other factors. The very area which is lacking may be the one which is confronted as the mission in life. In this concept, we attract what we lack. The missing element in our birth chart is provided by our partners, friends and family. The strange part is that we are often born to parents who astrologically provide the missing links. When we later leave the nest, it is common to seek the same link in our friends and partners. For example, people with little or no Fire signs in their charts will invariably attract Aries, Leo and Sagittarian people into their lives, regardless of whether they are ideally matched to Fire people. Similarly, people with an overload tend to attract people around them who will draw from their abundance and neutralise some of the potentially negative effects of the overload.

'Too much or too little' is of course a relative description, but five or more planets or points in the one element would be an overload; one or less indicates a deficiency. But if the one point in a particular element is the Sun, Moon, Ascendant or Midheaven (known as the 'personal' points), then it will carry additional weight and be far more significant than one of the outer planets in the deficient element.

As an interesting exercise, if you have an emphasis of two of the elements in your birth chart, for example Earth and Water, read the 'Mixing and Matching' comments for Earth and Water above. These are the joint energies operating within you, the individual, the motivating factors for your own unique power. Adapt to them accordingly.

TOO MUCH OR TOO LITTLE OF ONE ELEMENT — INTERPRETATION GUIDELINES

FIRE — AN ABUNDANCE: This overload can set the world on fire, but the urging, dynamic nature may be interpreted by some people as pushy or manipulative.

FIRE — A DEFICIENCY: Low energy and confidence levels, which must be sustained by plenty of affection and encouragement. There may be inadequate 'fuel' to burn up food quickly, making the selection of correct foods essential for good health.

EARTH — AN ABUNDANCE: This overload endows the individual with a closeness to Nature and the spiritual source. Rigidity of thought can lead to frugality with self and others. There is sometimes a limited imagination, but usually great discipline. Two significant examples of an Earth overload can be seen in the horoscopes of Father Teilhard de Chardin and Dr Louis Pasteur:

Father Teilhard de Chardin, a Jesuit priest who achieved worldwide acclaim for his scientific and genetic research, was born on 1 May, 1881, when seven of the twelve planets and points of his natal horoscope, including the Sun, were in Earth signs.

Dr Louis Pasteur was born on 27 December 1822, when eight of the twelve planets and points of his natal horoscope, including the Sun and Mercury, were in Earth signs (see Figure 2 for Pasteur's horoscope). Of these, Mercury, the Sun, Neptune, Venus and Uranus were all within a 7-degree conjunction in the sign of Capricorn; Mars was also in Capricorn. Under the Placidus system of house division, the whole planetary group was placed in the 3rd house of the Mind. An extraordinary mixture of energies for an exceptional man. The involvement of Neptune in the planetary combination suggests visionary qualities, psychic intuition and a deep personal belief system. Uranus adds revolutionary qualities, genius and determination to implement new dimensions of thought. The placement of the planetary

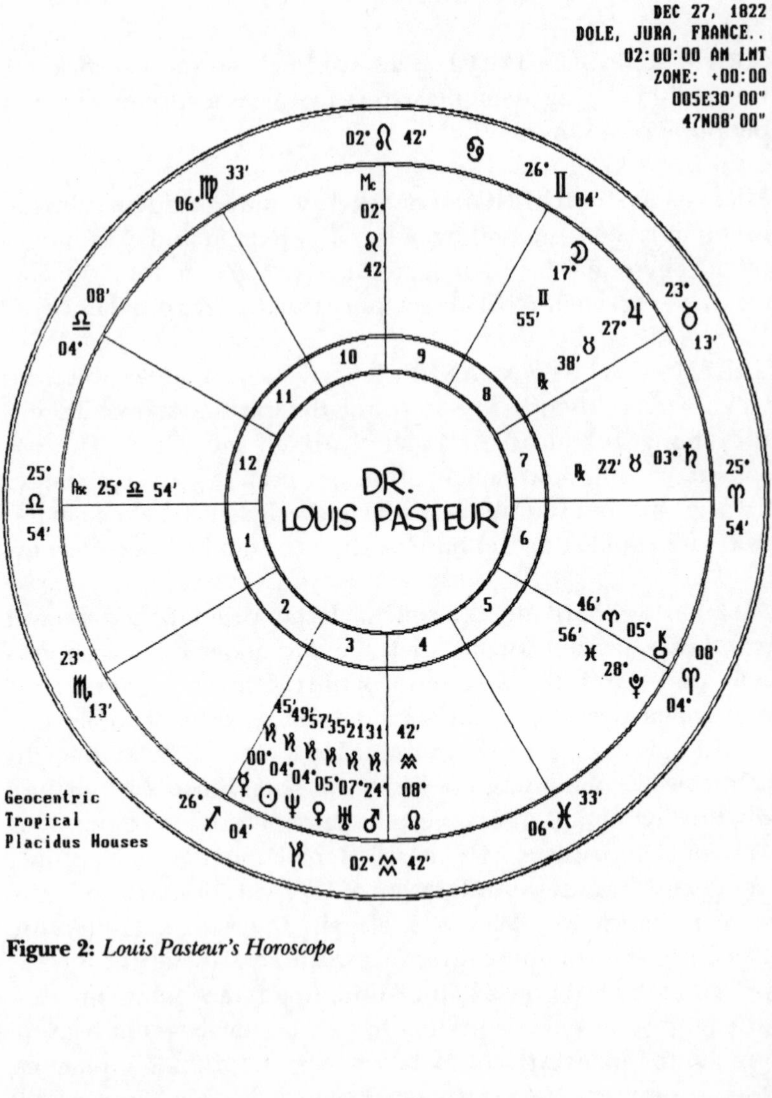

Figure 2: *Louis Pasteur's Horoscope*

group in the sign of Capricorn endowed Pasteur with a capacity to materialise his inspirations and make them accessible to humanity. The overload in Earth signs created gaps elsewhere and it is interesting that Pasteur has very little Fire and Water in his chart.

When reflecting on the charts of these two great ment, I think of them both as inspired realists.

EARTH — A DEFICIENCY

In his book *Astrology, Psychology and the Four Elements*, Stephen Arroyo states of people with too little Earth emphasis in the birth horoscope: –

> A 'lack of contact with the material world and with the physical dimension of reality can lead to the person feeling totally out of place in this world with no grounding or rootedness to provide him with support and solidarity in his efforts to express himself.'

I have heard it said that a lack of Earth coincides with a lack of financial ambition and material success. In some cases I have found the opposite to apply. The person with abundant Earth signs in the natal chart can usually achieve material comfort with relative ease, but those with a lack of Earth have a tendency to worry about security, often at the expense of other factors. There is frequently over-compensation; striving for emotional and material security becomes the major pre-requisite to happiness. Many low-Earth people look to the partners for security because it can sometimes be difficult for them to 'ground' their personal dreams single-handedly — but this is as it should be.

Two interesting examples of a lack of Earth in the birth horoscope are those of Edward, the Duke of Windsor, who was born on 23 June, 1894. Edward was a Cancerian with only one planet, Venus, in an Earth sign. Wallis Simpson, the Duchess of Windsor, was born on 19 June, 1895. Wallis was a Gemini, who had only one point, the Moon, in an Earth sign. Efforts to make tangible their ultimate life plan of marriage and the royal throne were not made easier by the fact that neither was an 'earthing' influence. Here we have both expressions of Earth deficiency operating. He sacrificed the power of the throne for the love of Wallis, placing higher value on the emotional security she offered. She looked to Edward for material and emotional security. Together they created a relationship which mystified and captured the imagination of millions.

In her book *Profiles of Women*, Lois M. Rodden gives the birth date of Wallis Simpson as 19 June 1896. However, Lois revised the date to 19 June, 1895 following the receipt of further information (*Mercury Hour,* July 1989). The 1896 birth chart for Wallis Simpson had no planets or points in Earth signs.

AIR — AN ABUNDANCE
Positively this can endow a person with brilliant mental faculties. Negatively, the over-emphasis on thought and reason can be at the expense of feeling and emotion.

AIR — A DEFICIENCY
People with little or no Air in their charts view life from their own unique perspective, which sometimes seems illogical to others, but which provides an abundance of warmth, feeling and frequently great benefits for those around them. Often the intellectual development becomes the challenge.

Stephen Arroyo maintains that low-Air people '… don't analyse themselves as a rule (unless Virgo is emphasised to off-set this) and they are rarely known for their reasoning power and articulate way of expressing themselves'.

Helen Keller was one of the most brilliant women of the century. Early illness left her a blind, deaf-mute, and yet she was able, with the help of her teacher Anne Sullivan, to communicate, speak and write. Helen Keller wrote many books and lectured in more than twenty-five countries. Born on 27 June, 1880, her birth horoscope had no planets or points in Air signs and it is possible that the lack of Air in her horoscope describes the enormous challenge communication would become to her. Born under the sign of Cancer, Helen had the Moon in Pisces, the Ascendant in Scorpio and Midheaven in Virgo (which provided the important reasoning power suggested by Stephen Arroyo above).

WATER — AN ABUNDANCE

Positively, abundant-Water people are renowned for their sensitivity, psychic gifts and natural ability to read and interpret the characters of others. Sidney Poitier, the award-winning actor who is well-known for his sensitive portrayals, was born on 20 February, 1927. His horoscope shows seven planets and points in Water signs, including the Sun, Mercury and Midheaven. Sidney Poitier is a living example of how positively a Water abundance can be expressed.

Negatively directed, a Water abundance is linked to hypersensitivity, defensiveness and a refusal to confront life, with subsequent escapism through drugs, alcohol or sickness as props. Sometimes those with abundant Water disguise their emotions in order to avoid vulnerability and consequently present a cold, detached image to others.

WATER — A DEFICIENCY

The lack of Water in the chart suggests a depletion of emotion, intuition and moisture. The Water-deficient individual may, however, seek partners who will reflect and express their own unexpressed emotions; this may be a conscious or unconscious action. Alternatively, emotionalism could be seen by the Water-deficient individual as a desirable trait.

Stephen Arroyo suggests that as Water is the healing and cleansing force, a lack of it usually results in a severe physical disturbance, due to an accumulation of toxins. But the intake of plenty of fresh springwater will wash away a multitude of dietary sins.

In closing, I wish to reiterate that a lack or abundance of any element in the birth horoscope is neither positive nor negative; it merely gives added focus and direction. It is the choice of the individual as to where the focus is directed. But as I mentioned earlier, these people usually make their presence felt in society.

QUINCUNX (OR INCONJUNCT) SIGNS — YOUR PARTNERSHIPS AND HEALTH

Those versed in astrology will be aware that when two planets are 150-degrees apart in the birth horoscope, they are said to be in Quincunx or Inconjuct. The Quincunx aspect is known as the 'health' aspect, because the 150-degree aspect is not a comfortable link. Consequently the planetary influences do not blend easily together, resulting in frustrating circumstances connected with the two planets involved.

When viewing the birth horoscope from the perspective of health, one has only to look to the physiological correspondences of the particular planets involved to evaluate potential vulnerability. For example if Mars (inflammations) was Quincunx to Saturn (the bony structure) in the chart, it is likely that there would be a propensity towards rheumatic-type conditions in that particular individual. On the other hand, that same person would probably be a hard worker, with an inclination to overextend his or her energy resources.

Australian astrologer Erik Holm states 'The two planets work, but they do not work together. The individual must construct the blend by learning through life', a philosophy which I believe could counteract many a health condition. In a 1984 lecture, American astrologer Alan Oken called the 150-degree aspect a 'neurotic' aspect. He reminded us that the word 'inconjunct' means 'doesn't quite make it'.

The Quincunx signs

I have examined the relationship between the zodiac signs which are 150-degrees apart, with a view to firstly determining the methods people born under these signs chose to unite and blend together, and secondly to apply them to the health of the individual. If physical and emotional conflict is to be avoided, we would be wise to understand and acknowledge the qualities of our Quincunx signs. It can readily be seen, when viewing these signs from the perspective of their element classifications, that they are not generally compatible. For example Aries (a Fire sign) is in Quincunx to Virgo (an Earth sign) and Scorpio (a Water sign).

Partnerships

Each zodiac sign has two Quincunx signs, one which activates a conscious reaction and one which activates a subconscious reaction. The conscious Quincunx of one sign is the subconscious Quincunx of the other, which means that both signs approach the relationship at a completely different level. Your relationship with your conscious Quincunx sign works on a logical, objective, but slightly critical level. Your relationship with your subconscious Quincunx sign operates on a deep feeling level, generating actions and responses from your spiritual centre which are often difficult for you and your subconscious Quincunx partner to understand. A subconscious Quincunx relationship is the most challenging and difficult to master.

It is possible to devise a successful formula for dealing with the 'rubber band effect', the compelling/repelling attraction generated by Quincunx action. We ultimately have the choice of learning from each other — through contrast or conflict.

Health

From the point of view of our health, the conscious Quincunx sign suggests health conditions which are obvious and externalised. A full understanding of your subconscious Quincunx sign may assist you to trace the underlying cause of a health condition.

If you are not well, perhaps by recognising and confronting these subconscious forces which can prove destructive to the relevant body areas, you can work to construct a satisfactory blend of energies.

Table of Quincunx signs

The following table lists the twelve zodiac signs, their associated Quincunx signs and related body areas. The comments after each sign may give some further insight as to the energies operating:

ARIES

Conscious Quincunx — *Virgo* … Lower intestines, digestion, constipation, hemorrhoids.
Subconscious Quincunx — *Scorpio* … Reproductive system, colon, prostate gland, bladder.

In some cases there may be a conflict between sexual motivation and puritanical conditioning.

TAURUS

Conscious Quincunx — Libra ... Kidneys, adrenal glands, acid-alkaline balance.

Subconscious Quincunx — Sagittarius ... Hips, thighs, liver.

With this group you must ensure that your desire to instill justice is not based on subjective idealism.

GEMINI

Conscious Quincunx — Scorpio ... Reproductive system, colon, prostate gland, bladder.

Subconscious Quincunx — Capricorn ... Knees, joints, teeth, gall bladder.

Attempts to surround the self with ardour and enthusiasm may stem from the need to bridge an inner gap.

CANCER

Conscious Quincunx — Sagittarius ... Hips, thighs, liver.

Subconscious Quincunx — Aquarius ... Calves, ankles and blood circulation.

You can be a great source of comfort and optimism to others provided you broaden your own horizons.

LEO

Conscious Quincunx — Capricorn ... Knees, joints, teeth, gall bladder.

Subconscious Quincunx — Pisces ... Feet, lymph glands, water retention, chemical imbalance.

Something seems to set you apart from others, despite your deep longing for tenderness.

VIRGO

Conscious Quincunx — Aquarius ... Calves, ankles and blood circulation.

Subconscious Quincunx — Aries ... Head, brain, blood pressure, stress.

You have something to give to everyone, but injustice can generate an angry fire within which is difficult to quell.

LIBRA
Conscious Quincunx — Pisces ... Feet, lymph glands, water retention, chemical imbalance.
Subconscious Quincunx — Taurus ... Throat, thyroid gland, liver/gall.

An impressionability may exist which must be confronted and overcome if you are to achieve the security you seek.

SCORPIO
Conscious Quincunx — Aries ... Head, brain, blood pressure, stress.
Subconscious Quincunx — Gemini ... Lungs, nervous system, hands, arms.

Instinct and intellect may clash. Channel your fire to give added momentum and inspiration to your intellectual ideals.

SAGITTARIUS
Conscious Quincunx — Taurus ... Throat, thyroid gland, liver/gall.
Subconscious Quincunx — Cancer ... Stomach, breasts, membrane coverings.

Despite your bid for freedom, something ties you eternally to your blood links. Your gourmet tastes can be your friend or foe.

CAPRICORN
Conscious Quincunx — Gemini ... Lungs, nervous system, hands, arms.
Subconscious Quincunx — Leo ... Heart, spine and back.

Whilst your duty lies in service to others, you are undoubtedly master or mistress of your own castle.

AQUARIUS
Conscious Quincunx — Cancer ... Stomach, breasts, membrane coverings.
Subconscious Quincunx — Virgo ... Lower intestines, digestion, constipation, haemorrhoids.

Your secure home is an essential base, provided an escape valve is available. Exercises of the mind are a fortunate diversion.

PISCES

Conscious Quincunx — Leo ... Heart, spine and back.
Subconscious Quincunx — Libra ... Kidneys, adrenal glands, acid-alkaline balance.

Your growl will become a whimper if you endeavour to sympathise with too many points of view. You can't please everyone.

Activation of the Quincunx signs

Your health and well-being are tested when the slow-moving planets transit your Quincunx signs. For example the Saturn/Neptune conjunctions in Capricorn in 1989 may have had important repercussions in the lives of Capricorns, but could also have generated reflex action in the lives and health of those born under the signs of Gemini and Leo — the Quincunx signs of Capricorn. Possible manifestations may have been stiffness of limbs and organ inflammation. For more on activation of the Quincunx signs, see Chapter 11.

Chapter Five

The Phases of the Moon

It would be possible to fill a book on the folklore surrounding the phases of the Moon. In the study of human nature, the reaction of human beings to the Moon phases is of particular interest. There is no argument about the fact that the Moon controls the ocean's tides. As our bodies are made up of 80 per cent water, it would be inconsistent to imagine that we are not susceptible to emotional fluctuation at certain periods during the phases of the Moon. In actual fact, many people are prone to physical and emotional highs and lows at the new and full Moon, which is quite feasible when we consider the cyclic effect the Moon cycles have upon birds, animals and plant life — why should we mere mortals be excluded from the laws of Nature?

The new Moon is a subjective period in the month, often associated with confused objectives. The Sun and Moon align in the same zodiac sign at the time of the new Moon.

Full Moons can generate the effect of a full tide within the body. Some people feel swamped, overwhelmed, unable to cope with existing conditions and are desirous of change. Others experience an exhilarating sense of joy and stimulation — a oneness with the Universe. The Sun and Moon are placed in opposite signs of the zodiac at the time of the full Moon.

The day of the full Moon is not an advantageous time to have an operation, due to an increased risk of haemorrhage. For more information see 'Timing the Operation' in Chapter 12.

THE LUNAR CYCLE AND HUMAN BEHAVIOUR

This is a controversial area. If more interest was shown in the effects of cycles, it may be possible to avert many tragedies. The full Moon frequently triggers crisis situations. Human response can be impulsive, erratic and actions ring of a conviction that the peak is 'here to stay'. Some seek support and understanding during the crisis, but others do not. Attention to the phases of the Moon would alert our senses. Knowledge provides a safety valve of tolerance and patience.

In the October 1984 edition of *Police Life*, the journal of the Victorian police, there is an article entitled 'Full Moon Phobias — Fact or Fantasy?' by Colleen Woolley. Many examples of crime associated with the full and new Moons are cited and one section confirmed much of what we counsellors hear first hand from those we meet who are working at the core of justice, viz ...,

> 'The Readers' Digest publication *Into the Unknown* states that it is a commonplace belief among police-men, firemen and ambulance drivers that their busi-est days — and more specifically nights — occur when the Moon is new or full, for those are the times when suicides, crimes of passion, arson and all manner of aberrant behaviour seem to crest.'

Australian astrologer Sandra Killin conducted a two year study entitled 'The Moon's influence on people involved in murder and murder-related suicides in Victoria Australia between 1983 and 1987'. She confirmed a high incidence of these crimes at the time of the full Moon, but discovered a surprisingly high inci-dence during the first and last quarter phases of the Moon.

THE MOON PHASES AND PERSONALITY TRAITS

Initially the Moon phases caught my interest because the mathe-matical relationships of the Sun to the Moon during all its phases coincides with the aspects emphasised in cosmobiology, my own special area of interest.

The Moon phases are as follows: –

New Moon = Sun conjunction Moon
Crescent phase = Moon 45-degrees ahead of Sun
First quarter = Moon 90-degrees ahead of Sun
Gibbous phase = Moon 135-degrees ahead of Sun
Full Moon = Moon opposition (180-degrees from) the Sun
Disseminating phase = Moon 135-degrees behind Sun
Last quarter = Moon 90-degrees behind Sun
Balsamic phase = Moon 45-degrees behind Sun.

The Moon was in one of these phases at the time you were born and regardless of what sign you were born under, the Moon phases coincide with distinct personality traits. It is necessary for you to know your Moon sign position as well as your Sun sign position in order to establish your personal Moon phase at birth.

Your local astrologer will provide this information.

For example, you are a new Moon type if you were born between the moment of the new Moon (Sun/Moon conjunction) until the Moon is 45-degrees ahead of the Sun; you are a full Moon type if you are born between the moment of the full Moon (Sun/Moon opposition) until the Moon is 135-degrees behind the Sun. Obviously there are varying degrees of intensity, but keep in mind that you cannot be a full Moon type until the full Moon has actually occurred, nor can you be a new Moon type if you were born the day before the new Moon. *The Lunation Cycle* by Dane Rudhyar is an excellent reference for those wishing to research the lunations further. Some of my observations agree with those of Rudhyar, others I have made during recent years of research. In keeping with the theme of this book, I have included comments relevant to the health of the individual.

New Moon types
(Moon conjunct Sun and less than 45-degrees ahead of Sun)
The most common traits attributed to new Moon types by astrological writers are subjectivity and confusion. I see these types as builders and visionaries, idealistic, optimistic and frequently motivated by a type of one-eyed enthusiasm. Confusion can exist between the ideal and the reality unless there are adequate Earth signs or other indicators of practicality in the natal chart. Alternatively, the support and guidance of practical people can prove invaluable. I believe such a close contact between Sun and Moon at birth results in a confusion, and often conflict, between the conscious and subconscious drives. New Moon people may feel compelled to partake of a high intake of fluids, highlighting the kidneys and water balance in the body.

Crescent types
(Moon 45-degrees and up to 90-degrees ahead of the Sun)
Rudhyar describes crescent types as 'assertive people with a karmic link to the past'. I believe crescent types are also clever, outspoken and success-orientated. It is feasible that these very qualities could attract the outside attack they are often subjected to. I would describe their links to the past as karmic debts. Former Indian Prime Minister Indira Ghandi was a crescent type.

The nervous system is linked to these Moon phase types.

First quarter types
(Moon 90-degrees and up to 135-degrees ahead of the Sun)
Self-motivation is the strongest trait of first quarter types. They usually demonstrate determination and force and have great potential for structured planning. My heart warmed to see so many successful, and frequently self-made women born under the phase, for example Queen Elizabeth II, Princess Grace of Monaco, Shirley McLaine, Barbra Streisand, Madame Curie and Germain Greer. The muscles and blood pressure are linked to these Moon phase types.

Gibbous types
(Moon 135-degrees and up to 180-degrees ahead of the Sun)
These types can be recognised through their high level of focus and obsessional traits. Obsessions can be beautiful; the gibbous type has an innate capacity to be a great contributor to humanity. There is often a quest for purity and a search for the source inherent in their nature. Prince Charles is a typical example of a gibbous type. The bony structure of the body is associated with those born under this Moon phase.

Full Moon types
(Moon 180-degrees [opposition] and up to 135-degrees behind the Sun)
I fully agree with Rudhyar that full Moon types are illuminated beings. He comments on an 'inner division — man against himself'. I believe this is because full Moon types see things as they are and want the rest of the world to share their enlightenment, which is why I call them the 'provocative intellectuals'. Unlike the new Moon type, which demands a blending of conscious and subconscious forces, the full Moon demands a confrontation of these forces. Inner conflict projected into relationships will test them to the limit. The greatest asset of full Moon types is their ability to motivate and activate others — consider the energy generated by Bob Geldof, Rudolf Steiner and Mata Hari, all full Moon types. The eyes, circulation and water balance are linked to these Moon phase types.

Disseminating types
(Moon 135-degrees to 90-degrees behind the Sun)
Rudhyar calls disseminating types the 'demonstrators and crusaders who have learnt their lessons through experience'. We could interpret this as hard times in childhood, or alternatively reactions stemming from deep within the psyche. Perhaps it is necessary for these people to resolve past life experiences. My research confirms Rudhyar's theory that they can be fanatical in their convictions and that they have the capacity to influence a large number of people. This trait can be inspiring if they have high principles, but destructive if they have immoral tendencies. My keyword for disseminating types is 'effectiveness'. Consider the extraordinary effectiveness of people like Marilyn Monroe, Helen Keller and Adolf Hitler, all disseminating types. The glands and reproductive system are associated with these Moon phase types.

Last quarter types
(Moon 90-degrees to 45-degrees behind the Sun)
Rudhyar describes last quarter types as 'inflexible reformers who challenge established belief systems'. I have noticed that last quarter types have a knack for generating a phase of self-assessment in the lives of those close to them. Their own lives and actions reflect vividly in the lives of others but such action is often met with resistance and antagonism by those who are unreceptive to change. Rudhyar suggests that last quarter types 'plant seeds for the future order'. This concept is confirmed when we reflect on the pillars of new thought bequeathed to humanity by Mahatma Ghandi and Carl Jung, both last quarter types. The blood and liver are linked to these Moon phase types.

Balsamic types
(Moon 45-degrees behind the Sun to the new Moon)
Balsamic types have a responsibility to humanity, which Rudhyar calls a 'social destiny'. They are mystical, sensitive, compassionate, and psychic and make excellent nurses, advisers and counsellors. They rely on a strong belief system and often attract to them people in unusual circumstances with unusual problems. Many balsamic types find their niche in alternative cultures and

lifestyles, breaking family traditions and creating new precedents. It is important for them to utilise their energies constructively, as they are deeply impressed and can be influenced detrimentally by those who appeal to their sense of the unusual — otherwise they can end up feeling a victim of circumstances. Psychiatrist Dr Elisabeth Kubler-Ross, who is famous for her work on death and dying, is a balsamic type. This Moon phase is associated with infections, allergies, the lymph glands and immune system.

THE SECONDARY PROGRESSED LUNATION CYCLE

Whilst the secondary progressions represent the complete horoscope in action, the secondary progressed lunation cycle is a valuable interpretative factor in itself. The days and months after our birth are said to symbolically represent the life tests and challenges we will confront; each day after birth is equivalent to one year of life. The manner in which we approach the life tests can be assessed through appraisal of the natal chart. Regardless of which cycle of the Moon you were born under, you will experience the energies of all cycles of the Moon in the 29.5 years of its progressed cycle.

The secondary progressed lunation cycle is too advanced for the purpose of this book, so I cannot examine it at length in this work, but its relationship to our state of health is undeniable. The period between the secondary progressed last quarter phase and the progressed new Moon is one of the most significant health factors of the cycle. This period, which lasts for approximately seven years, is about selectiveness and priorities, letting go of the past and concentrating upon that which is important. Those who ignore the warnings of their inner self and 'soldier on' are the ones most likely to fall prey to illness. The 3.5 year period between the progressed balsamic phase and the progressed new Moon is especially vulnerable; it should be a period of instinctive retreat and preparation for a new life path. Sensitive and aware people experience this as an enlightening period. I have confirmed the vulnerability level of this phase during recent years of discussion with students and clients, who provided information concerning their own lives. The balsamic factor is high on my list of periods of lowered resistance.

To a lesser extent, the progressed full Moon phase and many months before and after, can also be a period of vulnerability, as this is a time when the psychosomatic element assumes greater importance. Physical illness is possible unless the intensified emotions associated with this progressed phase are analysed and channelled constructively. Illusions are stripped away and life is presented to us in full spotlight.

Princess Diana of England was born with the Sun in Cancer and the Moon in Aquarius, when the Moon was within 18 minutes of orb of its exact disseminating phase. Despite the softening trine between the Sun and Neptune in her natal chart, Diana displays the crusading qualities of the disseminating type. The Sun's action-links to Venus, Uranus and her Aquarian Moon illustrate the original and independent nature which she displays. There is no doubt that Diana is highly effective in her role as a world trendsetter.

During her secondary progressed full Moon cycle, which became exact in August 1987, Diana would have seen some things more clearly and possibly concluded that, despite her efforts, her personal life was not living up to expectations. This phase coincided with her much publicised period of marital friction. Diana's birth horoscope indicates that her initial impulse would have been to rebel, but in the two years since then she has had time to absorb her impressions from that phase, learn from her experiences and get on with her life, a little older, but wiser. For readers with a more advanced knowledge of astrology, I have included Diana's cosmobiology chart in Chapter 14.

MOON PHASE DATES AND FERTILITY IN FEMALES

In past ages all women were closely in tune with Nature; artificial light and stimuli was non-existent and it is believed that the female menstruation and conception cycles were closely aligned with the phases of the Moon.

Czechoslovakian psychiatrist and gynaecologist, Dr Eugen Jonas, is known for his work correlating the human reproductive cycle with the lunar cycle. Dr Jonas concluded that a woman became fertile in each synodic lunar month when the Sun and Moon formed the exact relationship to each other as at the time of her birth. This occurrence is irrespective of her ovulation cycle and does not necessarily coincide with it. The theory implies that for some women there may be two fertile periods in one month — her ovulation date and her Moon phase date. If the ovulation and the Moon phase dates coincide, the woman's fertility is maximised. If, for no apparent physical reason, a woman is having difficulty conceiving a child, it is possible that her Moon phase date coincides with her menstruation. Dr Jonas cited examples of conceptions by women thought to be infertile, who had followed their Moon phase cycle in addition to their normal monthly ovulation cycle. Many women had conceived a child during menstruation. My own files contain several cases of women who have used this method and conceived on their Moon phase date.

MOON PHASE DATES AND BIRTH CONTROL

If fertility cycles can be accurately predicted, the obvious question arises — can completely accurate safe sex periods be predicted as an alternative to other contraception measures? I have had countless requests for lists of these dates from women who cannot take the pill. One request came from a woman who had already conceived twice whilst on the pill. Frankly I have not done enough personal research in the area of contraception to make a conclusive statement as to the effectiveness of this method as a contraceptive. The woman's individual fertility level is important and there are many other factors in astrology besides the phases of the Moon. I personally conceived my last child under strong Jupiter activation and if Jupiter was active during a 'safe' Moon phase period, I would be reluctant to rely on the Moon phase factor alone. Any woman wishing to experiment with this method should be prepared to treat it as an experiment only and not be too opposed to a conception. It will obviously work better for some women than others.

What of the fertility level of males during their monthly natal Moon phase? This is an unexplored area which could be of some interest as a research project to males who have a low sperm count.

THE SEX OF THE CHILD

Dr Jonas maintained that a second factor, the sex of the child, was related to the sign the Moon was in at the time of the woman's recurring monthly Moon phase. He claimed a high degree of accuracy in predicting the birth of male children conceived when the Moon was in the positive or masculine signs of Aries, Gemini, Leo, Libra, Sagittarius and Aquarius and female children conceived when the moon was in the negative or feminine signs of Taurus, Cancer, Virgo, Scorpio, Capricorn and Pisces. This is indeed a provocative theory. If in fact people could select the sex of their children and there was a greater demand for say, male children, the question of an imbalance of the sexes would obviously arise.

More information on the work of Dr Eugen Jonas is available in *Natural Birth Control* by Sheila Ostrander and Lynn Schroeder.

Chapter Six

Cycles of Health

The *World Book Dictionary* defines a cycle as 'Any period of time or complete process of growth or action that repeats itself in the same order'.

The *Larousse Encyclopedia of Astrology* defines a cycle as 'A regularly recurring period of time during which an event or series of events can be expected to occur and upon which predictions can be based'.

It is an accepted fact that our life is a cycle, and throughout our life span there are cycles which exist within cycles. How we take for granted the cycle of night and day, the cycle of the seasons — spring, summer, autumn and winter — the cycles of conception, birth, life and death.

All cycles have a beginning, a waxing or expanding period, a culmination point of awareness, a waning period of decreasing momentum and an end. The waxing half of the cycle symbolises gathering and growth whilst the waning half of the cycle symbolises release and reaping. The planetary cycles are sound indicators as to the prevailing conditions in our life at a given time. Our life events, successes and failures, depend on how we deal with the cycles, not upon the cycles themselves.

All cycles are rhythmic and powerful. The power of the lunar cycle can influence the tides. Next time you are beside the ocean, observe the rhythm of the waves. Liken the commencement of a cycle to the point when the wave has withdrawn, leaving the sand exposed. As a new wave gathers momentum, it increases in energy, force and power, which we could liken to a waxing motion. As the wave crashes to the beach and floods the sand, it represents the culmination of the cycle — all-engulfing and emotional, with potential for crisis. As the wave gradually draws back, it can be likened to a waning cycle, reclaiming its forces and power, taking with it some of the flotsam from the shore and conserving its strength for the next wave.

THE PROGRESS OF A CYCLE

Waxing

From a personal point of view, the start of a cycle can represent the commencement of a new concept, career, lifestyle or relationship. As we move through the waxing half of a cycle, our new life gathers momentum and we valiantly defend our cause against all manner of opposition. As we approach the culmination of the cycle, the flooding generates emotional repercussions and a heightened awareness, which results in a questioning of our original aims. Occasionally our cause is aborted within the waxing period, depending upon the strength of our initial direction.

Waning

During the waning part of the cycle the original aim has either been restructured into a modified form, or it will gradually disperse to be replaced by new aims as the cycle ends. During waning we spiritually reap the harvest of what we have sown during the waxing phase. As the universal power reclaims its forces, it is necessary for us to discriminate, cling to what is important and discard what is irrelevant or which belongs to the past. The final stage of the waning phase is a period of vulnerability and preparation for the commencement of the next cycle. This is a period of true wisdom. If we have acquired humility during the course of the cycle, we will discover our true needs, which are frequently quite different to the needs which fired our imagination at the commencement of the cycle. During the final stage of the cycle we will discover who our true friends are and best of all, who we are.

In this chapter we will discuss the fast-moving points in the horoscope — the Sun, Moon, Mercury, Venus and Mars. Their cycles recur frequently in our lives, but they are nonetheless important. In chapters 7, 8 and 9 we will deal with the slow-moving planets Jupiter, Saturn, Uranus, Neptune and Pluto. Large numbers of people are born whilst a slow-moving planet is in a particular zodiac sign, which is why astrologers refer to them as the 'generation' planets. People of the same age will share generation cycles together, for example people aged between twenty-eight and thirty would have many experiences and impressions to exchange in a 'Saturn Return Club'.

THE SOLAR, LUNAR AND FAST-MOVING PLANETARY CYCLES

Most Western astrologers use the geocentric, or Earth-centred, system of astrology. As the reader will be aware, the Earth is but one of the stellar bodies travelling around the Sun. (See Figure 3 'The Solar System').

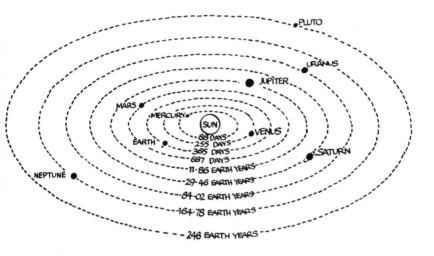

Figure 3: *The Solar System*

For our purpose, a planetary cycle is a period in our life when a planet has completed an orbit around the Sun and returned to the exact position it was in the zodiac at the moment of our birth. Although the Sun and Moon are not planets, some information on the solar and lunar cycles has been included in this section. It is helpful to know your exact planetary birth positions, or birth horoscope, and facilities for obtaining these are included at the end of this book in the bibliography.

It is necessary to refer to the *Ephemeris* (astrologer's book of planetary positions) or a professional astrologer if you wish to determine the exact dates of the solar, lunar, Mercury, Venus and Mars returns during your life. However, in the case of the slow-moving planets Jupiter, Saturn, Uranus, Neptune and Pluto, it is possible through understanding the length of the cycles to assess your age at the time of activation. With this book and little or no knowledge of astrology, you can evaluate the effectiveness of the slow-moving planets by comparing their periods of activation with your life events.

Not all the slow-moving planets will complete a cycle in your lifetime. Neptune for example, takes 164.78 years to complete an orbit around the Sun and unless someone discovers the elixir of youth, we will never experience a Neptune return. Pluto takes 248.4 years to complete a cycle through the zodiac. I have included sections on both planets as both are vital to medical astrology.

However, we do experience regular solar, lunar, Mercury, Venus, Mars, Jupiter and Saturn returns. A Jupiter return occurs every 11.86 years, a Saturn return every 29.46 years, and some of us will experience a Uranus return at 84 years of age. Although the focus of this book is on health, we must not ignore the whole perspective of our lives. Sound health, life experiences and personal philosophy are closely intertwined.

The return of the Sun — your solar return ☉
The great journey of the Earth around the Sun will place the Sun annually in the same position of celestial longitude as it was at the moment of your birth. The solar return chart is calculated for the time the Sun is placed in its exact point with reference to the fixed stars, that it held in your birth chart. This will occur annually on your birthday, the day before or the day after. The moment of your solar return varies from year to year.

It is common for highly significant events of a positive or negative nature to occur on, or within days, of the birthday. How many times have you read in your newspaper that Miss Y was competing in the Olympic Games on her birthday, or that Mr Z had a major accident and would have been 'X' years old the next day? The solar return is a peak — the commencement of your new solar year.

In other words, the qualities of the moment of your annual solar return are said to indicate the flavour of the year ahead. Around the time of their birthday, many people take on a new lease of life and make 'new year' resolutions concerning their relationships, lifestyle and health regime. The Sun represents the life force and vitality; the solar return indicates potential for strength, or lack of it, in the year ahead.

Many astrologers are superstitious regarding their activities at the time of the solar return. Some believe that pleasant surroundings and good company at this time will stimulate good tidings for the year ahead. This is not surprising when we consider the superstitions prevailing annually on 31 December, the calendar new year.

The solar return is calculated for the location you are at when the solar return occurs. This means that by relocating to another place, your prognosis for the year ahead may improve. As a professional astrologer, I have had several people seeking consultation who are prepared to spend money travelling a specific distance in order to have a more auspicious solar return chart for the year ahead. Personally I do not allow astrology to influence my own life to that extent.

The month immediately prior to your birthday represents the end of the previous solar cycle. It is the psychological cleansing and preparation phase, so it is not unusual to experience a lethargic lull and lowered resistance during this month. Use the time wisely to reflect, meditate and gain momentum for the new cycle. A cleansing diet will expedite spiritual progress. Some readers may be helped by the suggestions I have made on diet and nutrition under the Leo section of Chapter 11.

To find life examples of the solar cycle in operation, we have only to look to our own lives and those of our family and friends. In astrology we learn by observation.

Anna Pavlova, one of the world's greatest ballet dancers, was born in Leningrad, Russia on 31 January, 1882 — a true Aquarian, with the Sun, Mercury and Venus in the sign. Originality, determination and self-will are three of the most dominant traits of Aquarius, traits which helped Pavlova break new ground in the world of dance and share her extraordinary talent and passion for dancing with the world at large. She travelled the world, spreading beauty and inspiration wherever she went.

Because of her relentless personality, Pavlova did not allow herself rest when she was tired or ill. After rehearsing in an unheated studio, on 17 January, 1931, she became ill from a lung inflammation. In the month prior to her birthday, instead of reflecting and preparing for the coming year, she embarked on a new tour to Holland. She died in Holland on 23 January, 1931, one week before her birthday, dancing almost until the day she died. Naturally there were other astrological factors involved; this is one of them. For Pavlova's birth horoscope see Figure 4.

The 31 January 1882 birthdate used for Pavlova's chart is from the Russian edition of her husband's biography of her (Encyclopaedia Brittanica). Other sources give 31 January 1881 as Pavlova's birthdate, when the Sun, Moon and Mercury were in Aquarius. Either example will illustrate Pavlova's vulnerability immediately prior to her birthday.

☽ THE RETURN OF THE MOON — YOUR LUNAR RETURN

The Moon moves rapidly through the zodiac. The lunar return occurs every 27.32 days, when the Moon returns to the exact point it held, with reference to the fixed stars, that it held in your birth chart. However, because of the apparent motion of the Sun, 29 days, 12 hours, 44 minutes and 3.0 seconds elapse between one new Moon and the next (also known as the synodic month). Do not confuse the lunar return with the synodic month.

It is interesting that the Moon's cycle is similar to the normal female menstrual cycle. The Moon governs our moods, emotions and bodily fluids. Those who are sensitive and easily upset, physically and emotionally by external influences, would benefit from studying their lunar return cycle, as it is possible, through greater understanding, to adjust one's responses. Many people suffer from catarrh and disorders of the stomach and eyes, or experience a fluctuating water balance at the time of their lunar return and this can be adjusted through the use of natural substances. (For more information see the section on the sign of Cancer in Chapter 11).

In his book *Solar and Lunar Returns*, Donald A. Bradley states that the lunar return is essentially a health chart for the month ahead, which will be effective until the next lunar return. We are all aware of the high level of variability which exists from month to month, within a given year and the lunar return chart is a sound indicator as to when additional preventative measures are required.

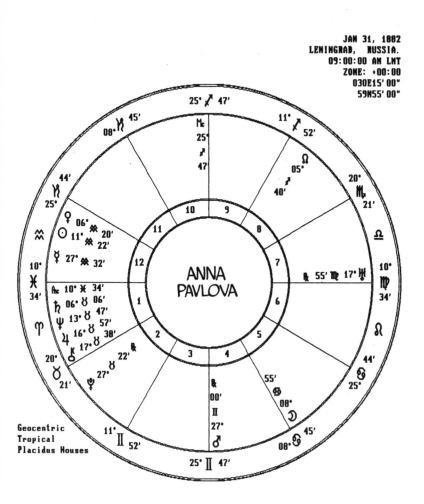

Figure 4: *Anna Pavlova's Horoscope*

Your Mercury return ☿

Of the nine major planets, Mercury is the closest to the Sun. Although its sidereal period is approximately 88 days, its geocentric revolution is variable and closer to one year in length. Mercury has recurring periods of apparent retrograde motion, which means that if Mercury in transit turns retrograde when it is close to your Mercury birth position, you will experience more than one Mercury return within a short space of time.

The Mercury return chart will provide information as to the current state of your nerves and the dexterity of the communication systems within your body such as hearing, sight, speech and physical mobility. If you experience some restriction or disability in these areas, it should be apparent in your recent Mercury return charts. If there is a nervous reaction during the period of your Mercury return, adjustments to your lifestyle or the inclusion of dietary supplements may be necessary. For more information, read the Gemini and Virgo sections of Chapter 11.

Your Venus return ♀

Venus is the second planet in order of distance from the Sun and is larger than Mercury or Mars. Although its sidereal period is 225 days, its geocentric revolution is variable and closer to one year in length. Venus turns into its apparent retrograde motion every 1.5 years, which means that if Venus in transit turns retrograde when it is close to your Venus birth position, you will experience more than one Venus return within a short space of time.

Classically, Venus is the relationship planet, ruling love, pleasures and the social aspects of life. The Venus return chart can also give some indication as to the current state of your glands, hormones, throat, thyroid and kidney functions. At the time of the Venus return several of the Venus functions may be linked — the hormones, reproductive system and love/relationship factor can relate to the birth or conception of a child. Parenting is a popular expression of the Venus return.

A classical example is Princess Diana of England, whom we discussed in Chapter 5. Although Diana is a Cancerian, born on 1 July, 1961, Venus was placed at 24 degrees 25 minutes of Taurus when she was born. Her first-born son Prince William, is also a Cancerian, born on 21 June, 1982. When William was born,

Venus was placed at 25 degrees 39 minutes of Taurus. In other words, Venus was within about a degree of where it was placed when Diana was born. When William was born Diana was having a Venus return. You can read more about these family links in Chapter 13 'Astro-Hereditary'.

Some Venus returns can activate an imbalance in the glands, hormones and reproductive system, depending upon the birth chart and other astrological factors in operation at the time. For more information on helpful lifestyle adjustments and dietary supplements, see the Taurus and Libra sections in Chapter 11.

Your Mars return ♂

Mars is the first of the superior planets, lying beyond the orbit of the Earth. Its period of revolution is 687 days. Mars represents our desires, goal directions, sexuality and aggressions. As it rules the muscles, adrenal glands, blood, acidity, fevers, inflammations, eruptions and burns, the return of Mars to its natal position can give some indication as to the current condition of these functions. The Mars return is also helpful for determining periods of being accident-prone and the circumstances which surround operations planned for the months ahead, that is, up until the next Mars return.

Of all the astrological techniques available to astrologers, correct interpretation of the birth horoscope is the single most important factor. You must have an accident-prone birth horoscope in order for a major accident to occur. At some time in our lives, we are all subject to an operation, however minor in nature. If an operation is pending, your current Mars return chart gives helpful guidelines concerning your energy and recuperative powers — this includes elective surgery as well as emergency surgery. Information on timing the operation is available in Chapter 12, 'The Onset of Illness'.

Each Mars return heralds the commencement of your new biennial 'energy' cycle. It will indicate the manner in which you will take action, initiate and instigate new projects. The Mars return is important to those who rely on a high output of energy: sportsmen and women in training, business executives and young mothers with active toddlers are three groups of people who immediately spring to mind.

As discussed above, a particularly difficult Mars return, which is indicated by the birth chart in relation to the other astrological factors operating at the time, can be associated with a phase of energy depletion. In the Aries section of Chapter 11, 'Personal Depletion Factors', I have included some helpful guidelines.

Chapter Seven

Cycles of Health — Jupiter and Saturn

♃ CYCLES OF JUPITER

Jupiter is the largest planet in the solar system, its mass and volume being greater than all the other planets put together. It rotates faster and has the shortest day of the planets, which is 9 hours 50 minutes long. Astrologers often refer to Jupiter as the great benefactor, with 'larger than life' effects.

Jupiter is accredited with philosophical, expansive and protective qualities and yet it can be activated in the horoscope during times of major upheaval. It appears to be the great exaggerator, magnifying both positive and negative potential; it can generate hope and faith for the insecure and yet cultivate foolhardy over-confidence in the self-assured. Jupiter's protection has an affinity with 'good luck', so that lottery wins are often accompanied by Jupiter activation.

JUPITER RETURNS

The Jupiter cycle is known as the 'cycle of opportunity'. Jupiter takes 11.86 years to return to the point in the zodiac where it was placed at your birth and will therefore return to its own place at approximately 12, 24, 36, 48, 60, 72 and 84 years of age, give or take a year. The Jupiter return is usually, although not always, associated with hope and enthusiasm: many people have an urge to expand their lives through new career and environmental options in the years of their Jupiter returns; others choose to bond with another in marriage, a live-in relationship or through parenting a child. The confidence to sow new life-seeds becomes evident.

JUPITER/SUN-SIGN ACTIVATION

Approximately one in twelve people have Jupiter in the same zodiac sign as their Sun sign at birth, but the other eleven will have Jupiter in a different sign. Both the positive and negative effects of Jupiter can be experienced when Jupiter moves through your Sun sign, in its continuous journey through the heavens. Although this occurs at approximately twelve year intervals, the age of individuals when Jupiter moves through their Sun sign is variable.

Extraordinary events have been known to occur when Jupiter activates the Sun sign. Our ideals and self-confidence are frequently reinforced, but sometimes instead of the reassurance we have been led to expect from many astrological textbooks, we are tested to the limit. We may enjoy overseas travel, astral travel and great financial gains, but also great financial losses. There is often an important legal matter: a contract may be signed to enhance lifestyle, but occasionally there is legal conflict.

Many experience a link with the infinite; it is not uncommon to receive news of a death, although not necessarily that of a close relative. Despite the sadness involved, physical death can be interpreted as a state of expanded consciousness. The person dying often has a far more positive horoscope at the time than those left behind to deal with the loss.

JUPITER CYCLES AND YOUR HEALTH

As a general rule, the Jupiter return coincides with improved health and vitality. The illnesses of Jupiter are associated with the liver, blood, over-indulgence, poor fat absorption and general weight problems. You will become more susceptible to the illnesses of Jupiter at the time of your Jupiter returns and especially when Jupiter transits your Sun sign. The placement of Jupiter in your birth horoscope in relation to the other planets must also be taken into consideration; such individualised detail cannot be included in these simplified explanations.

Below is a table of all the zodiac signs, with approximate periods Jupiter was placed in each sign since late 1921. Because of the retrograde motion of Jupiter in geocentric astrology, it is often placed in a sign for additional short periods at the beginning or end of the longer placement in that sign. For more detailed information refer to *The American Ephemeris for the 20th Century* by Neil F. Michelsen, or consult a professional astrologer. If using the table below, evaluate Jupiter's action by determining activation periods in your life as follows: –

Your Jupiter return
Check through the dates to establish which zodiac sign Jupiter
was in when you were born. Then check the subsequent dates
Jupiter was in that sign for the periods of your Jupiter return
action.

Jupiter in your Sun sign
Most readers will know their birth sign or Sun sign. If not, refer
to Chapter 3. Find your sign below and check the dates Jupiter
was in that sign for the periods of your Jupiter/Sun sign action.

Reminisce and recall your experiences during both cycles.
They should give you first-hand knowledge of the Jupiter effect,
the great benefactor and exaggerator of life. Consider your state
of health during both cycles. Rather than merely assess the
events which occurred, try to recall your outlook and determine
whether there were any consistencies of attitude or similar life
themes in subsequent cycles. From my own experience, Jupiter
seems to bestow an abundance, but frequently 'too much' to
deal with. If Jupiter has brought you pain, he will eventually
bestow benefits and broaden your horizons.

TABLE OF JUPITER IN THE TWELVE ZODIAC SIGNS
ARIES
June to September 1927, January to June 1928.
May to October 1939, December 1939 to May 1940.
April 1951 to April 1952.
April 1963 to April 1964.
March 1975 to March 1976.
March 1987 to March 1988.
February to June 1999, October 1999 to February 2000.

TAURUS
June 1928 to June 1929.
May 1940 to May 1941.
April 1952 to May 1953.
April 1964 to April 1965.
March to August 1976, October 1976 to April 1977.
March to July 1988, December 1988 to March 1989.
June to October 1999, February to June 2000.

GEMINI
June 1929 to June 1930.
May 1941 to June 1942.
May 1953 to May 1954.
April to September 1965, November 1965 to May 1966.
August to October 1976, April to August 1977, December 1977 to April 1978.
July to November 1988, March to July 1989.
June 2000 to the 21st century.

CANCER
June 1930 to July 1931.
June 1942 to June 1943.
May 1954 to June 1955.
September to November 1965, May to September 1966, January to May 1967.
August to December 1977, April to September 1978, March to April 1979.
July 1989 to August 1990.

LEO
July 1931 to August 1932.
July 1943 to July 1944.
June to November 1955, January to July 1956.
September 1966 to January 1967, May to October 1967, February to June 1968.
September 1978 to February 1979, April to September 1979.
August 1990 to September 1991.

VIRGO
August 1932 to September 1933.
July 1944 to August 1945.
November 1955 to January 1956, July to December 1956, February to August 1957.
October 1967 to February 1968, June to November 1968, March to July 1969.
September 1979 to October 1980.
September 1991 to October 1992.

LIBRA
September 1921 to October 1922.
September 1933 to October 1934.
August 1945 to September 1946.
December 1956 to February 1957, August 1957 to January 1958, March to September 1958.
November 1968 to March 1969, July to December 1969, April to August 1970.
October 1980 to November 1981.
October 1992 to November 1993.

SCORPIO
October 1922 to November 1923.
October 1934 to November 1935.
September 1946 to October 1947.
January to March 1958, September 1958 to February 1959, April to October 1959.
December 1969 to April 1970, August 1970 to January 1971, June to September 1971.
November 1981 to December 1982.
November 1993 to December 1994.

SAGITTARIUS
November 1923 to December 1924.
November 1935 to December 1936.
October 1947 to November 1948.
February to April 1959, October 1959 to March 1960, June to October 1960.
January to June 1971, September 1971 to February 1972, July to September 1972.
December 1982 to January 1984.
December 1994 to January 1996.

CAPRICORN
December 1924 to January 1926.
December 1936 to December 1937.
November 1948 to April 1949, June 1949 to November 1949.
March to June 1960, October 1960 to March 1961, August to November 1961.

February to July 1972, September 1972 to February 1973.
January 1984 to February 1985.
January 1996 to January 1997.

AQUARIUS
January 1926 to January 1927.
December 1937 to May 1938, July to December 1938.
April to June 1949, November 1949 to April 1950, September to December 1950.
March to August 1961, November 1961 to March 1962.
February 1973 to March 1974.
February 1985 to February 1986.
January 1997 to February 1998.

PISCES
January to June 1927, September 1927 to January 1928.
May to July 1938, December 1938 to May 1939, October to December 1939.
April to September 1950, December 1950 to April 1951.
March 1962 to April 1963.
March 1974 to March 1975.
February 1986 to March 1987.
February 1998 to February 1999.

5 CYCLES OF SATURN

The size and mass of Saturn is inferior only to Jupiter. Its elaborate ring system adds to the mystique and beauty of the planet. A full cycle of Saturn, or its return to the position in the zodiac it occupied at birth, takes 29.46 years. The cycles of Saturn are extremely effective and many astrologers believe they are the greatest astrological prognosticators. To the ancients, Saturn was the outermost planet; Saturn reinforced their belief in the inevitability of time.

SATURN RETURNS

Depending upon the life span, we may experience three Saturn returns — at 29, 58 and 87 years of age. The first cycle, between birth and 29 years, is the cycle of personal learning and the gathering of experience. The second cycle between 29 and 58 years represents the individualised expression of life. During the second cycle we strive to establish ourselves; many purchase a home, raise a family, climb the career ladder and fulfil their ideals through achievement. The third cycle, which is the period between 58 and 87 years, is ideally a life cycle to cater for the higher self. Finally there is the time, and hopefully the resources, to reflect, improve the education, focus on spiritual development and travel further afield in order to increase the wisdom and life experiences.

These three phases frequently overlap. Many of our greatest conflicts occur when we refuse to move from one cycle to the next. For example, some people at 29 years do not wish to take responsibility for their own life and actions. Others may wish to broaden their lifestyle but have a spouse who regards the 'new independence' as a threat to the relationship. Either way, the result can be a conflict which often leads to a separation. The first Saturn return calls for a reassessment of values and priorities. The relevance of one's own choices, as distinct from choices made to comply with the wishes of others, assumes a new urgency.

Initial effectiveness

The initial effectiveness of the first Saturn return becomes apparent prior to 29 years, and usually as early as 28 years of age. Some people are not unduly ruffled by their first Saturn return; others have a complete change of lifestyle. It can be extremely positive for those who feel a greater sense of commitment and responsibility to themselves and others. Many marry, have a rise in status or a promotion in their career.

The age of 58 marks the second Saturn return and once again the approaching phase of reassessment is felt in the year prior to the return. This cycle represents the opportunity to break down the doors of self-discovery leading to the higher dimensions of self. But instead of moving forward, many grieve for the past. Why dwell on the family which has grown up and left home, the career which is fading, the relationship which is no longer exciting? Endeavour to enrich your own life. The real loss is to waste these valuable years; what at first appears to be an ending, is actually a beginning.

SATURN SUB-CYCLES

Saturn forms four 7-year sub-cycles within its 29-year cycle. These are especially apparent during the formative years of 7, 14, 21 and 28 to 29. Positive and negative growth experiences occur during these sub-cycles. As the sub-cycles repeat themselves in the second major cycle, it is interesting to observe how the ages at recurrent sub-cycles interconnect. For example, Saturn is opposite its natal position, or halfway through the cycle, at 14 years of age. Following the first Saturn return at 28 to 29 years, Saturn forms its second opposition sub-cycle at 42 years. Unresolved emotional and physical problems from the 14th year can resurface as the sub-cycle repeats itself in the 42nd year. From a positive perspective, 42 is an ideal age to confront that which we couldn't deal with at 14. At 42 we have the power, experience and wisdom to reclaim our lost ideals, without running away. (Figure 5 illustrates two complete cycles of Saturn with linking sub-cycle periods).

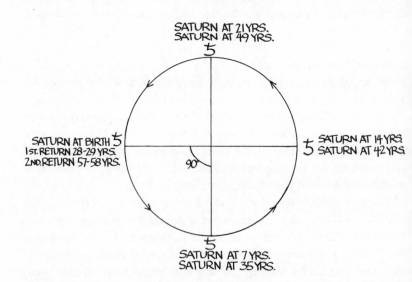

Figure 5: *The 7-year Saturn Sub-Cycles*

The early to mid-40s is a popular period to recapture youthful experiences, often at the expense of home and family. Although

Saturn action has the potential to make us feel a failure, Saturn's discipline can help us to restore our aspirations, beautiful body and good health to their former glory. Saturn has not been labelled the 'Teacher' without good reason. Properly applied, the Saturn cycles can help us to fully understand our strengths and limitations and utilise that which is ours alone.

In *Cycles of Becoming*, a comprehensive study of planetary cycles as they relate to human development, Alexander Ruperti states:–

> '... *most people think of a cycle simply as a repetitive eternal return to the same starting-point. If a cycle is reduced to a closed circle of repetitive events, it cannot have the creative, evolutionary meaning it possesses when understood to be the expression of a creative process.*'

SATURN/SUN-SIGN ACTIVATION

Approximately one in twelve people have Saturn in the same zodiac sign as their Sun sign at birth, but the other eleven will have Saturn in a different sign. At some stage in the first 29 years of your life, Saturn will pass through your Sun sign. The most outstanding manifestation of Saturn's movement through your Sun sign is an increasing desire to make a commitment, take on a responsibility and 'earth' oneself. Saturn can highlight what we fear most, so that security becomes a priority. It can slow down or restrict our progress, so that we have to work harder to achieve our goals. The activation of Saturn frequently coincides with separations. Saturn also has an affinity with politics, government personnel, senior officials and the elderly.

As the Sun represents our physical vitality, Saturn action to the Sun can place restrictions on our strength — Saturn transits are high on my list of periods of lowered resistance. But it seems that when the average person is faced with Saturn transits they realise that something must be done immediately to maintain their vitality. I became aware of this fact when I was driving through early-morning Melbourne on my way to the radio station where my astrology segment had been broadcast for the previous two years. The Sun and Saturn were in alignment on the day, so the vibration was generalised. I expected as usual, to see deserted streets, but instead it seemed that half the population of

Melbourne was out jogging, not in one group but in random groups, scattered through the city.

SATURN CYCLES AND YOUR HEALTH

The cycles of Saturn can activate chills, cramps, calcification and sluggishness in the body. The teeth, bones and skin are often the first areas where Saturn action is evident. Saturn is symbolised by 'Old Father Time'; Saturn action can make you feel older, more tired and stiffer. Many people experience periods of temporary or extended depression — 'the pain they cannot explain'. It has been said that apart from drug therapies, exercise is a popular cure for breaking the vicious depression cycle. Exercise therapy is also beneficial for combating the blocking/inhibiting effects of Saturn. Exercise stimulates the circulation and breathing mechanism, getting us moving and motivated again.

Saturn remains in each zodiac sign for approximately 2.5 years. Below is a table of all zodiac signs with the approximate periods Saturn was placed in each sign since 1920. Because of the retrograde motion of Saturn in geocentric astrology, it is often placed for additional short periods at the beginning and end of its longer placement in a zodiac sign. For more detailed information refer to *The American Ephemeris for the 20th Century* by Neil F. Michelsen, or consult a professional astrologer. If using the table below, evaluate Saturn's action by determining activation periods in your life as follows: –

Your Saturn return

Check through all the dates to establish which zodiac sign Saturn was in when you were born. Then check the subsequent dates Saturn was in that sign for the periods of your Saturn return action.

Saturn in your Sun sign

Find your Sun sign and check the dates Saturn was in that sign for the periods of your Saturn/Sun-sign action after your birth year.

Recall your experiences during these cycles. In retrospect, did Saturn live up to its reputation of being the 'Teacher', and more importantly, did you mature and become a better person through your experiences?

Table of Saturn in the Twelve Zodiac Signs

ARIES
April to October 1937, January 1938 to July 1939, September 1939 to March 1940.
March 1967 to April 1969.
April 1996 to June 1998, October 1998 to March 1999.

TAURUS
July to September 1939, March 1940 to May 1942.
April 1969 to June 1971, January and February 1972.
June to October 1998, March 1999 to the 21st century.

GEMINI
May 1942 to June 1944.
June 1971 to January 1972, February 1972 to August 1973, January to April 1974.

CANCER
June 1944 to August 1946.
August 1973 to January 1974, April 1974 to September 1975, January to June 1976.

LEO
August 1946 to September 1948, April to May 1949.
September 1975 to January 1976, June 1976 to November 1977, January to July 1978.

VIRGO
August 1919 to October 1921.
September 1948 to April 1949, May 1949 to November 1950, March to August 1951.
November 1977 to January 1978, July 1978 to September 1980.

LIBRA
October 1921 to December 1923, April to September 1924.
November 1950 to March 1951, August 1951 to October 1953.
September 1980 to November 1982, May to August 1983.

SCORPIO

December 1923 to April 1924, September 1924 to December 1926.
October 1953 to January 1956, May to October 1956.
November 1982 to May 1983, August 1983 to November 1985.

SAGITTARIUS

December 1926 to March 1929, May to November 1929.
January to May 1956, October 1956 to January 1959.
November 1985 to February 1988, June to November 1988.

CAPRICORN

March to May 1929, December 1929 to February 1932, August to November 1932.
January 1959 to January 1962.
February to June 1988, November 1988 to February 1991.

AQUARIUS

February to August 1932, November 1932 to February 1935.
January 1962 to March 1964, September to December 1964.
February 1991 to May 1993, June 1993 to January 1994.

PISCES

February 1935 to April 1937, October 1937 to January 1938.
March to September 1964, December 1964 to March 1967.
May to June 1993, January 1994 to April 1996.

Chapter Eight

Cycles of Health — Uranus ♅

Uranus was discovered in 1781 by William Herschel, as he was surveying the sky with a 150-millimetre reflector. Many astrologers believe that as a new planet is 'discovered', knowledge of its existence coincides with the surfacing of a new-life spectrum in the consciousness of humanity: the discovery of Uranus coincided with the Industrial Revolution. In the horoscope, Uranus is associated with inventiveness and innovation.

THE 84-YEAR URANUS CYCLE

The Uranus cycle is often known as the 'cycle of change'. Slow-moving Uranus takes 84 years to complete its cycle and return to the point in the zodiac where it was placed at your birth. Uranus has magical qualities — a type of 'now you see it, now you don't' effect on our lives. I liken Uranus action to a bold of lightning. Words like sudden, unexpected, rebellious and revolutionary' are often used to describe the Uranus effect.

Physiologically, Uranus is associated with a cerebral form of nervous energy. The mental vibrations are so fast that the person born with Uranus strategically placed in the birth horoscope will find it difficult to switch to conventional learning modes, or alternatively will be far ahead of the group. Either way, both types will approach life in a different manner to the average person.

The 84-year Uranus cycle is remarkable in that it can be likened to a complete life span, although many people live much longer than 84 years of course. The 84 years can be subdivided into: –

Twelve 7-year cycles (Uranus takes approximately seven years to move through each zodiac sign)

Seven 12-year cycles (which coincide with the cycles of Jupiter)

Three 28-year cycles (which coincide with the cycles of Saturn).

URANUS CYCLES AND YOUR HEALTH

Because of the erratic and unexpected nature of Uranus, health crises are not uncommon at four major periods in the cycle, that is at the age of 21, 42, 63 and 84. Naturally much will depend on the individual constitution, inherited health tendencies and lifestyle as to what type of condition could manifest. However, the nervous, cerebral and coronary functions are particularly susceptible for some people. Spasms and twitches can also be linked to Uranus energy. Alternatively, these life phases may coincide with periods of great restlessness and change, exciting events and positive decision-making. The full natal horoscope will provide the clues.

At 21 years of age Uranus is in a waxing square (90-degrees ahead) of its birth position; at 42 years of age Uranus is opposite its own birth place; at 63 years of age Uranus is in its waning square (90-degrees behind its birth position); at 84 years of age Uranus returns to its position at your birth. (Figure 6).

THE 84-YEAR URANUS HEALTH CYCLE DIVIDED INTO TWELVE 7-YEAR SUB-CYCLES

Regardless of what zodiac sign Uranus was in at the time of your birth, each 7-year cycle after birth can be symbolically linked to a zodiac sequence. Do not confuse these 7-year cycles with the sign Uranus was actually in at birth or when you were say, 0 to 7 years old. This theory is symbolic in that the 0—7-year-old period has a distinct Aries flavour, the 7—14-year-old period has a distinct Taurus flavour, etc.

Much work has been done on cycles by Alexander Ruperti in his book *Cycles of Becoming* and by the famous astrologer Dane Rudhyar. I have adapted these cycles to include my own findings and viewed them predominantly as cycles of health, incorporating physical development with psychological factors.

As discussed earlier in Chapter 2, the use of polarities or opposite signs in our interpretations is essential. For example, when considering the throat and thyroid of Taurus, we must also consider the reproductive and eliminative systems of the opposite sign of Scorpio and vice versa. Figure 6 illustrates the twelve 7-year Uranus health cycles, with opposite polarities well defined.

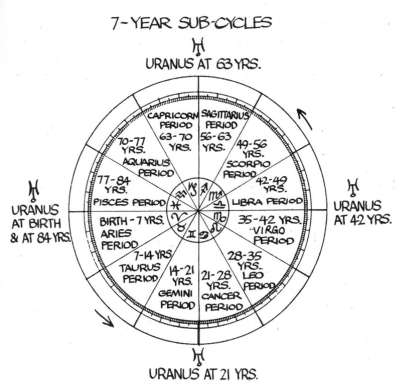

Figure 6: *The 84-year Uranus Health Cycle*

0 – 7 years (the Aries-Libra sub-cycle)

The period of adventure and self-discovery, when accidents in the form of bumps to the head, burns, bruises and cuts are common. Focus on the kidneys and bladder during toilet training can include problems with bed-wetting and good judgment by the parents is essential during this phase. There is a fine line between the freedom to explore and satisfy curiosity and the personal safety of the child. Too much discipline during toilet training will lead to rebellion and possible health conditions of the urinary tract and bowels at a future date. First friendships are formed. The child starts to relate and learn that there are others beside himself or herself.

7 – 14 years (the Taurus-Scorpio sub-cycle)

A period of semi-obsessions, manifesting in popularisation of activities and 'crazes' at school — swap cards, hoops, best friends, pop stars, television idols and fad foods being some of the manifestations. Transference, possessiveness and destructive behaviour such as nail biting are other examples of the intensity felt by the child during this phase. The mouth, throat, neck, tonsils, excretory and developing reproductive system will be areas of sensitivity and possible fascination. It is important for the child to learn to share, but also to feel secure and loved.

14 – 21 years (the Gemini-Sagittarius sub-cycle)
During this phase the young person is heavily involved in communication and social interaction. The nervous system, hands, arms, shoulders, lungs, sciatic nerve, hips, liver and hormone balance are the body areas highlighted. The mental acumen is tested through learning, writing, reading, competing and playing. Sport, dance and music can play a positive recreational role and add balance to overstressed nervous systems. It is not uncommon for young people to suffer from nervous exhaustion and strain, or injury to the limbs during this phase. Adequate sleep and a nourishing diet will help avoid depressed states and depletion factors.

21 – 28 years (the Cancer-Capricorn sub-cycle)
This is a phase of nurturing. Many people parent a child or establish their own 'nest'. However it can represent a conflict between the parent and child within each of us. Ideally it is a time of 'emotional weaning' from parental dominance, which can be achieved in a friendly or unfriendly manner, depending upon the strength and adaptability of the parental influence. Those who do not take some control of their own destiny during this phase will be the losers and may harbour resentment in later life.

The stomach and digestion, gall bladder, metabolism, breasts, skin, bony structure and teeth are highlighted during this phase. We are prone to emotionalism and subjectivity; many people seeking answers to emotional issues over-indulge in substitutes such as food and alcohol.

We must be objective if caught up in a difficult situation — life requires work and effort. If necessary counsel should be sought from rational friends, relatives and professional advisers.

28 – 35 years (the Leo-Aquarius sub-cycle)

This vital period of life centres around ambition, vocation, personal effort, individuality and a strong contribution to a life shared with others. There will be a tendency to overdo things.

The back, heart, circulation, calves and ankles are the vulnerable areas at this time, although generally the health and recuperative powers are good. Sporting enthusiasts will enjoy great strength and a heightened competitive spirit.

It is easy to feel invincible at this time, and it should be remembered that wise choices must be made and sensible priorities be taken into consideration.

35 – 42 years (the Virgo-Pisces sub-cycle)

Physically the food tolerance levels are tested during this phase. Many people automatically reassess their dietary needs and health in general and take positive steps to adjust their lifestyle in accordance with their changing bodily requirements.

Mentally it is a period of discrimination. Our likes and dislikes are carefully examined, but nevertheless, we may do some of our most outstanding work.

The digestive tract, spleen, lymphatic system, nervous system and feet may be the underlying cause of health problems at this time. Potential food and chemical allergies as a possible source of any discomfort and unpleasant symptoms experienced should be investigated. It is important to find a personal level of exercise to calm nerves and eliminate dissatisfaction. Yoga can be extremely beneficial.

42 – 49 years (the Libra-Aries sub-cycle)

This significant phase, often labelled the 'mid-life crisis', can involve a throwback to our childhood days. The age of 42 years heralds the commencement of the externalisation of the wisdom we have gleaned since birth. If we were spoilt and given free rein during our period of freedom and self-discovery (0 – 7 years), it will be harder to adapt to others' needs at this time. Many people choose to break away and do things *their* way. All relationships are tested and many break; sometimes past relationships are revived. Adaptability is the only way to go during this phase, especially if peace of mind is to be retained.

The kidneys, hormone balance, acid/alkaline balance, blood pressure and cerebral function are stressed. Conditions such as insomnia, headaches, dizziness and neuralgia can be helped with the right treatment. The flesh and skin will start to lose tone, but exercise will keep the muscles and organs firm.

49 – 56 years (the Scorpio-Taurus sub-cycle)

Complex feelings can accompany this period of changing life function. Whilst the 7—14-year-old period is concerned with the developing reproductive system, the 49—56-year-old is concerned with stabilising the reproductive system and generally marks the end of the female reproductive cycle.

The obsessions and security consciousness depicted between the ages of 7 and 14 can once again manifest as possessiveness, a fear of ageing and an obsession with one's sexual prowess, or lack of it.

The reproductive system, bowel, bladder, throat and neck are the areas requiring preventive measures in the form of diet and attitude.

Productive career outlets, hobbies and family involvement can provide the necessary outlets for health and happiness.

56 – 63 years (the Gemini-Sagittarius sub-cycle)

This period has the potential for being extremely social and highly rewarding for the individual involved in living life to the full. It is an excellent phase to share the wisdom of your experience with younger friends and family members, as you will be a natural 'teacher' at this time.

Many people in this age group are inspired to travel and consider alternative study options and some may exercise their writing skills and be published. Others, unfortunately, will become bored and restless, develop high cholesterol levels and weight problems, nervous anxiety, disorders of the blood and liver and stiffness in the hips and back.

During these years a re-focus of personal potential is essential. It is important to live an active and useful life, or we may conclude that we have outlived our usefulness. In many cases the children have left the home and parents in this age group frequently experience a void. Creative hobbies involving use of the brain and hands will avoid negativity. A written account of life experiences will be treasured by later generations.

63 – 70 years (the Cancer-Capricorn sub-cycle)

This period can represent a peak of achievement, the crowning glory of a life's work. Many people are still in a productive work phase, but others will retire and seek an alternative occupation or interest.

During these years we reap our health harvest, which is based on how we have treated our bodies in the preceeding 63 years. The effects of calcification and hardening of joints and arteries may require attention. Common manifestations are stones in organs such as kidneys and gall bladder, hardening of the joints and arteries, drying of skin and scalp and loss of teeth and hair.

Between the ages of 21 and 28 it is necessary for us to emotionally establish our own individuality. Between 63 and 70 it is time to 'let go' of others and allow them to grow. It may be hard to accept, but we could unwittingly restrict and hinder the potential of those we love most. The crystallising effect of our personal life at this time can be interpreted by others as rigidity, and it is important to physically and emotionally 'loosen up'. Natural remedies are readily available to ease discomfort. Oils, massage, exercise, all forms of lubrication, fresh air, natural surroundings, the garden and scenic enjoyment will help eliminate apprehensions during this phase.

70 – 77 years (the Leo-Aquarius sub-phase)

New ambitions and motivations appear during this phase. Sometimes there is a loss of the partner so it becomes important to involve oneself in groups of people in order to establish new friendships and develop new interests. Unexpected happiness is possible if we take a positive approach to our circumstances and seriously consider the contribution we can make to those who will eventually take our place. Many couples in this age group acquire a refreshing incentive to share new hobbies, courses and activities involving intellectual stimulation. Lack of effort can promote poor circulation, lessened muscle co-ordination and absent-mindedness.

The blood pressure, vascular system, legs, ankles, back and

heart are vulnerable areas on which to concentrate healing and
preventative measures.

77 – 84 years (the Virgo-Pisces sub-cycle)
Individuals in this age group have a tendency to withdraw unless
established in a positive routine of interests, friends and family.
This is a period of reflection, acceptance, sentiment and spiritual understanding. Sometimes it is hard for the younger generation to see through the crusty veil often reflected by age because
it is frequently disguised by ill health, plus a spirit which is still
young and resents the limitations of an ageing body.

Through illness, many people lose their independence and
are hospitalised or placed in accommodation centres for the
elderly. A strong input of love and encouragement from others
becomes increasingly important to the elderly person. In return
they will impart the wisdom they have drawn from their reservoir
of life experience and family history. Those in this phase are our
teachers of life.

The 77-to 84-year-olds should adhere to dramatic dietary
modification, especially in the quantity of food consumed —
toxic effects are likely through malabsorption of food. The bladder and general vitality are weakened; foot complaints such as
bunions are common. Fresh fruit and vegetables and easily
digested nutrients, combined with purified water, can revive,
restore and cleanse the body.

84 years and later
Those reaching this major milestone will have a new lease of life.
I have heard stories of relocation and even remarriage at this
time. The seven-year cycles repeat themselves in what could only
be described as a second childhood or at the very least a 'second
wind'. The age of 84 years commences the second Aries-Libra
sub-cycle.

URANUS/SUN-SIGN ACTIVATION
Approximately one in twelve people have Uranus in the same
zodiac sign as their Sun sign at birth, but the other eleven will
have Uranus in a different sign. Both the positive and negative
effects of Uranus can be experienced when Uranus moves

through your Sun sign, in its continuous journey through the heavens after your birth.

Because Uranus takes 84 years to complete a full cycle through the zodiac, some people may never experience the effect of Uranus moving through their sign. But if not, most will have equally dynamic experiences as Uranus moves through their opposite sign.

Despite the fact that Uranus takes approximately seven years to move through each zodiac sign, and may take many years into your particular sign to reach your exact Sun sign degree, you will notice the seeds of restlessness manifesting shortly after Uranus enters your sign — a type of premonition of changes to come. You will adopt increasingly independent attitudes and have sudden urges to make changes in your environment and relationships. Alternatively, you may attract these influences, almost like a magnetic force, whereby those close to you play out the Uranus factors as the cause, and you experience the effects. It can be an exciting period, but can also be quite dramatic. Unexpected events, meetings and separations are possible.

As Uranus moves through their Sun sign, many people are drawn to public life and adopt a high profile position. Uranus rules the sign of Aquarius; you may therefore generate an Aquarian 'flavour' and either meet Aquarians or attract many friends and multi-associates into your circle.

Below is a table which indicates the approximate periods Uranus has moved through each zodiac sign since 1904. Check to see if Uranus has moved through your Sun sign since you were born. If so, ascertain what you learnt from Uranus, the 'Great Innovator'.

Because of the retrograde motion of Uranus in geocentric astrology, it is often placed in a sign for additional short periods at the beginning or end of the longer placement in that sign. For more detailed information refer to *The American Ephemeris for the 20th Century* by Neil F. Michelsen, or consult a professional astrologer.

URANUS IN YOUR OPPOSITE SIGN

As discussed above, the slow movement of Uranus through the zodiac means that it may not have appeared in your sign since long before your birth and may not return to your sign until well into the 21st century. Why not examine the years Uranus was in your opposite zodiac sign? It is an interesting exercise. In this case the Uranus effect will still be prominent — especially with regard to your relationships. The same excitement and changeable circumstances will make it an unsettled, but memorable seven-year period.

THE HEALTH FACTORS
URANUS IN YOUR SIGN OR OPPOSITE SIGN

The nervous, cerebral and coronary functions discussed earlier will also apply when Uranus moves through your Sun sign or opposite sign. Accelerated nervous conditions can often be mistaken for coronary disorders and vice-versa and regular medical check-ups will avoid confusion and worry.

Table of Uranus in the twelve zodiac signs from 1904 to the 21st century

ARIES
Entry April 1927, Longest placement January 1928 to June 1934, Exit March 1935.

TAURUS
Entry June 1934, Longest placement March 1935 to August 1941, Exit May 1942.

GEMINI
Entry August 1941, longest placement May 1942 to August 1948, Exit June 1949.

CANCER
Entry August 1948, Longest placement June 1949 to August 1955, Exit June 1956.

LEO
Entry August 1955, Longest placement June 1956 to November 1961, Exit August 1962.

VIRGO
Entry November 1961, Longest placement August 1962 to September 1968, Exit June 1969.

LIBRA
Entry September 1968, Longest placement June 1969 to November 1974, Exit September 1975.

SCORPIO
Entry November 1974, Longest placement September 1975 to February 1981, Exit November 1981.

SAGITTARIUS
Entry February 1981, Longest placement November 1981 to February 1988, Exit December 1988.

CAPRICORN
Entry and Longest placement December 1904 to January 1912, Exit November 1912.
Entry February 1988, Longest placement December 1988 to April 1995, Exit January 1996.

AQUARIUS
Entry January 1912, Longest placement November 1912 to April 1919, Exit January 1920.
Entry April 1995, Longest placement January 1996 to well into the 21st century.

PISCES
Entry April 1919, Longest placement January 1920 to March 1927, Exit January 1928.

Chapter Nine

Cycles of Health – Neptune and Pluto

♆ NEPTUNE

The planet Neptune was first sighted by the German astronomers Johann Galle and Heinrich d'Arrest in 1846, after years of observation and speculation. Prior to the actual sighting, the British astronomer John Couch Adams had plotted Neptune's position, based on discrepancies in the orbit of Uranus. (Who of us can forget 25 August 1989, the day when the spacecraft *Voyager* approached the glowing blue atmosphere of Neptune, revealing its secrets and resolving some of the myths surrounding it?)

The discovery of Neptune in 1846 coincided with the romantic age of music. Spiritualism and hypnotism grew and religion was a compulsory part of life. The spiritual aspect of astrology gained momentum and the oriental concept of karma and rebirth was incorporated into Western astrological thought. Medically the discovery of Neptune coincided with the use of ether anaesthesia, which was publicly administered for the first time in 1846.

The symbol of Neptune represents the human spirit transcending the physical factor, the cross of matter and the earthing of spiritual aspirations.

As the ruler of Pisces, Neptune denotes physical and emotional sensitivity, impressionability, compassion and confusion. The Neptune effect can dissolve reality and diminish feelings of self-worth, but it can also give the individual a capacity to sublimate pride and ego consciousness into a form of inspired creativity and ecstasy.

In his book *Astrology Karma and Transformation*, Stephen Arroya demonstrates his remarkable insight into the symbolism of the planets. On Neptune, Stephen Arroya states: –

> *To me, the most useful way of describing Neptune's essential meaning is to say that it represents the urge to lose one's self in another state of consciousness (whether 'higher' or 'lower' consciousness) and the urge to escape from all limitation, from*

both the limitations of material existence and its boredom and
the limitations of the personality and ego. Naturally one can
seek to escape through either self-destructive or personally con-
structive activities.'

Whilst Neptune is frequently prominent in the horoscopes of
spiritual and creative leaders, it can also bring fame and
notoriety. Prominently Neptune individuals are those most
likely to be allergic to chemicals, stimulants and spirits, but often
are those most likely to be attracted to them.

Actress Marilyn Monroe was a Gemini with the Moon in
Aquarius. She was born on 11 June, 1926 at 9.30 a.m. in Los
Angeles, USA. At this time of day on 1 June in 1926, Neptune was
rising in Leo. Marilyn was endowed with all the magical, techni-
colour qualities of Neptune, but also its mystery and vulnerability. Despite her rise to fame, her short life was full of personal
disappointment. Even the last hours of her life are shrouded in
mystery. Since her death, the enigma of her life has developed a
web of folklore and fascination. Her name, still conjures up the
nostalgia of years gone by — the 'Golden Years' of Hollywood
stardom.

THE HEALTH FACTORS OF NEPTUNE

Individuals with a prominent Neptune in their birth horoscopes
are born under all zodiac signs. From the health perspective,
Neptune is associated with weakness, slackness of function and
tone, paralysis, the pineal gland and the lymphatic system. It can
relate to toxic substances in the body, which undermine the
health on many levels.

Unless an astrological comparison can be arranged between
doctor and patient, Neptune people must rely on their intuition
to ensure they select a compatible health practitioner. It is possible for incompatible practitioners, through no fault of their
own, to misread their patient, resulting in misdiagnosis and the
wrong treatment. I personally believe we are drawn to the right
people at the right time, but at the wrong times, awareness,
precaution and confidence in personal judgement are essential. Those dissatisfied with their progress should seek a
second opinion.

NEPTUNE SUB-CYCLES

Neptune takes 164.78 years to complete a circle around the Sun and, unless someone discovers the elixir of youth, we will never experience a Neptune return. However, the Neptune sub-cycle is highly effective. If we live to be 82 years, we will experience Neptune in opposition to its natal position (the position it was placed in when you were born).

At approximately 20 years of age — Neptune is in a waxing semi-square (45-degrees) to its birth position.

This phase represents changing values and priorities, and efforts to establish material and emotional security, which are often thwarted. Youth strengthens resistance to disease, but this can still be a period of lowered physical and emotional resistance, depending upon personal stamina and other factors in the birth chart.

41 to 42 years of age — Neptune in a waxing square (90-degrees) to its birth position.

This is a period of changing tastes, which can include tastes in relationships. It is the truly adult phase of taking responsibility for one's actions whilst being haunted by unresolved ghosts from the past. Many people become acutely aware of the biological clock. If your life has 'begun at 40', it is due to your own insight and the fact that you have dared to unlock your innermost feelings and deal with them. The digestive system takes on a new meaning, especially for those who have been indiscriminate in their thirties; in many cases, adjustments must be made. Some people become allergy-prone and familiar substances are often the cause.

61 to 62 years of age — Neptune in a waxing sesquiquadrate (135-degrees) to its birth position.

Whilst this can be a personally creative period, it will serve as a constant reminder to physically and emotionally 'loosen up'. In some instances it is necessary to loosen the hold on adult children who may be struggling to refine their own identities and succeed in their own right. The heart, back and cerebral function will offer warning signs to those in the 61 to 62 years age group who choose to waste energy remaining focussed in their past roles. Such an exercise can be physically and emotionally draining and worst of all, uncreative.

82 years of age — Neptune in opposition to its birth position.

This phase of sensitivity and increased spiritual awareness can coincide with a period of lowered resistance. Susceptible astrological and hereditary body areas become prone to disease and infection. This period can be accompanied by a loss of confidence in self and others and a lull in the fighting spirit. It can also be a rewarding life phase, provided support and encouragement are offered by younger family members; the phase can last for up to two years.

NEPTUNE THE GENERATION PLANET

Neptune remains in a zodiac sign for approximately fourteen years, which becomes a common factor for a whole generation of people born during those years. For example, Neptune was placed in the sign of Virgo during the following periods: –

September 1928 to February 1929, July 1929 to October 1942 and April to August 1943.

If you were born during these periods, your intestines should not be neglected, regardless of what time of year or Sun sign you were born under. Those born at this time lived through a changing awareness of dietary fashion and suffered the effects of ill-informed dietary habits, but many from this generation have been the instigators of the New Age of Nutrition. As a result of the hardships of the Depression and the commencement of World War II, this group grew up under a nutritional economy, which later generations of the Western world have not yet experienced.

NEPTUNE/SUN SIGN ACTIVATION

Approximately one in twelve people have Neptune in the same zodiac sign as their Sun sign at birth, but the other eleven will have Neptune in a different sign. Both the positive and negative effects of Neptune can be expressed when Neptune moves through your Sun sign after birth, in its continuous journey through the heavens. As mentioned earlier, Neptune takes approximately fourteen years to move through one zodiac sign, so that only a limited number of people will experience this effect. Some believe that the birth date and time is chosen by the soul in order to experience a specific spiritual destiny during the lifetime.

The Neptune experience is quite profound and those who have lived it will recall a period lasting approximately two years within the fourteen-year span, when the sensitivity and confusion of Neptune manifested. Some may have conquered the vulnerability and reached new spiritual heights; others could have fallen prey to illness and disappointment. The desire to 'escape' is usually prominent. There are very positive forms of escape and activities such as travel, art, music, painting and writing, which should be explored. Water and oil have healing properties during Neptune activation and all types of water therapy, oil baths, massage, swimming, fishing and boating are positive channels for Neptune energy.

NEPTUNE IN YOUR OPPOSITE SIGN

As discussed above, the slow movement of Neptune through the zodiac means that it may not have appeared in your sign since long before your birth and may not return to your sign until well into the 21st century. In this case, it is likely that Neptune will move through your opposite sign during your lifetime, coinciding with a long period of confusion in your relationships. If you are already in a relationship, under Neptune activation it will be difficult for you to be definite about the direction the relationship will take. You may attract Neptune types of people, that is medical, musical, mystical, sensitive or vulnerable types. A touch of intrigue will surround one aspect of your life.

Below is a table which indicates the approximate periods Neptune has moved through specific zodiac signs since 1901. For your Neptune/Sun sign action, see if Neptune has or will move through your sign or opposite sign during your lifetime. If action has already occurred since your birth, ascertain what you learnt from Neptune, the 'Great Sensitiser'. Because of the retrograde motion of Neptune in geocentric astrology, it is often placed in a sign for additional short periods at the beginning or end of the longer placement in that sign. For more detailed information refer to *The American Ephemeris for the 20th Century* by Neil F. Michelsen, or consult a professional astrologer.

Table of Neptune in the zodiac signs from 1901 to the 21st century
CANCER
First entry July 1901, Longest placement May 1902 to September 1914, Exit May 1916.

LEO
First entry September 1914, Longest placement May 1916 to September 1928, Exit July 1929.

VIRGO
First entry September 1928, Longest placement July 1929 to October 1942, Exit August 1943.

LIBRA
First entry October 1942, Longest placement August 1943 to December 1955, Exit August 1957.

SCORPIO
First entry December 1955, Longest placement August 1957 to January 1970, Exit November 1970.

SAGITTARIUS
First entry January 1970, Longest placement November 1970 to January 1984, Exit November 1984.

CAPRICORN
First entry January 1984, Longest placement November 1984 to January 1998, Exit November 1998.

AQUARIUS
First entry January 1998, Longest placement November 1998 to April 2011, Exit February 2012.

NEPTUNE AND CHILDHOOD SENSITIVITY
As discussed in other sections of this book, geocentric astrology,

which is practised by the majority of astrologers, is a system of Earth-centred astrology. Because Earth is only one of the heavenly bodies moving around the Sun, the planets periodically appear to move into a retrograde motion. It is common for a slow-moving planet such as Neptune to change its apparent direction from direct to retrograde soon after the birth of a child, in which case Neptune will return to its natal position within months of the birth.

Depending upon the child's birth horoscope and whether he or she has a propensity towards a specific illness, the retrograde Neptune soon after birth may indicate a period of vulnerability. Keep in mind that the Neptune placement is only one of the factors considered by the astrologer.

Case history

Ben was born on 15 December, 1981 in Victoria, Australia, a bright and healthy boy. His Sun sign at 23 degrees 19 minutes Sagittarius was little more than 1 degree from Neptune, which was placed at 24 degrees 32 minutes Sagittarius. It could be said that the strong musical thread which ran through the family would predominate in Ben's life. But the Sun represents the life force, and its alignment with Neptune suggests that at certain periods during Ben's life he would have a significant change of energy levels and a lowered resistance towards disease. Neptune was in direct motion at his birth and moved to 27 degrees 02 minutes Sagittarius before it went into retrograde motion on 29 March, 1982.

Ben was a much-loved child, but in June 1982 he caught a common cold from which he did not recover and investigations revealed that he had a bone marrow deficiency. The fight to save him was fierce; his initial six months of good health made it all the more difficult for his family to accept his illness. Ben's last weeks were spent in an intensive care ward and despite a bone marrow transplant, he died in his mother's arms on 7 July, 1982, the day after the total eclipse of the Moon. Neptune was at 25 degrees 08 minutes Sagittarius, having moved back to within close proximity of its natal position, reinforcing the sensitivity of the birth chart and magnifying its effectiveness. As stressed above, the Neptune factor is only one of those considered in the assessment of the health signs. Figure 7 illustrates Neptune's retrograde motion between Ben's birth and death.

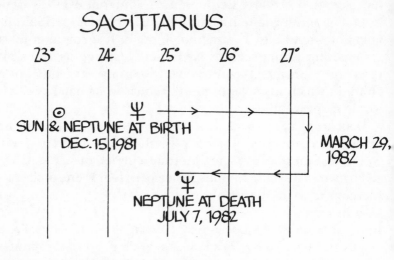

Figure 7: *Ben – Neptune's Direct & Retrograde Motion*

♇ PLUTO

In the early part of the 20th century, American astronomer Dr Percival Lowell concluded that the orbits of Uranus and Neptune were being affected by a more distant, but unknown planet. Lowell died in 1916. It was not until 1930, using improved equipment, that Clyde Tombaugh discovered the planet, which was named Pluto after the Greek God of the Underworld.

Pluto has an extremely erratic orbit and is regarded as an enigma by the scientific world. The fact that this apparently tiny planet could create gravitational effects on much larger planets remains controversial — and yet astrologers have always associated Pluto with power and transformation. When Pluto was discovered, the world was still suffering from the Great Depression, criminal activity was acute, Hitler was working towards his bid for world power, atomic energy was being developed and the antibiotic drug was on the horizon.

THE HEALTH FACTORS OF PLUTO

Pluto rules the sign of Scorpio, the reproductive, eliminative and defence systems. American medical astrologer Mary Vohryzek maintained that Pluto is associated with allergic reactions (my own personal research agrees with Mary's findings). Eileen Nauman links Pluto to enzyme production and the endocrine system.

Pluto governs birth, death and rebirth, obsessions, the subconscious mind, psychoanalysis and the collective unconscious, although the latter also has strong links with Neptune.

THE PLUTO CYCLE

Pluto's cycle through the zodiac takes 248.4 years. The eccentricity of Pluto means that it does not remain in any one zodiac sign for a consistent period, making it difficult to research the subcycles in the simplified manner of the other slow-moving planets. During the 20th century Pluto is placed in Gemini, Cancer, Leo, Virgo, Libra, Scorpio and Sagittarius. The following table gives some indication as to Pluto's variability. Because of the retrograde motion of Pluto in geocentric astrology, it is placed in a sign for additional shorter periods at the beginning and end of the longer placement in that sign. For more detailed information refer to *The American Ephemeris for the 20th Century* by Neil F. Michelsen, or consult a professional astrologer.

Table of Pluto in the zodiac signs from 1882 to the 21st century

GEMINI
First entry 1882, Longest placement May 1884 to September 1912, Exit May 1914.

CANCER
First entry September 1912, Longest placement May 1914 to October 1937, Exit June 1939.

LEO
First entry October 1937, Longest placement June 1939 to October 1956, Exit June 1958.

VIRGO
First entry October 1956, Longest placement June 1958 to October 1971, Exit July 1972.

LIBRA

First entry October 1971, Longest placement July 1972 to November 1983, Exit August 1984.

SCORPIO

First entry November 1983, Longest placement August 1984 to January 1995, Exit November 1995.

SAGITTARIUS

First entry January 1995, Longest placement November 1995 to January 2008, Exit November 2008.

THE PLUTO EFFECT

A major crossroad and life reassessment occurs when Pluto forms its waxing square to its position at birth. But there is no consistent year of age when the phenomenon occurs. The following examples will give the reader some idea of the variables: —

Those born with Pluto in Gemini would have experienced a reassessment when Pluto was in Virgo. (For example, someone born in 1900 will experience the Pluto effect at the approximate age of 64 years.)

Those born with Pluto in Cancer would have experienced a reassessment when Pluto was in Libra. (For example, someone born in 1926 will experience the Pluto effect at the approximate age of 52 years.)

Those born with Pluto in Leo will experience a reassessment while Pluto is in Scorpio. (For example, someone born in 1948 will experience the Pluto effect at the approximate age of 41 years.)

Those born with Pluto in Virgo will experience a reassessment when Pluto is in Sagittarius. (For example, someone born in 1963 will experience the Pluto effect at the approximate age of 36 years.)

Pluto activation marks a period of beginnings and endings involving home and career and your past and future acquaintances. If the health is effected it will be as a result of sheer pressure, either from outside circumstances or generated from within yourself. Subconscious emotions which stem from past conditioning must be confronted as Pluto energy endows a sense of force, urgency and fatality. In some cases a pending psychological crisis requires professional guidance.

PLUTO IN YOUR SUN SIGN AND OPPOSITE SIGN

The slow movement of Pluto means that only certain zodiac signs will experience Pluto moving through their Sun sign or their opposite sign during their lifetime. Examine the list above to see if Pluto moves through your sign or your opposite sign. If not, your local astrologer will advise you regarding Pluto activation in your birth chart. There are many different techniques and perspectives used in the complete horoscope which cannot be included in these simplified explanations.

If you do experience Pluto/Sun sign activation during your lifetime, your intensity will increase over a two-year period, possibly to the point of obsession. You may rise and fall from power or become involved in power struggles on behalf of yourself or others. Life will be black or white; there will be no half measures. If you do harness the power of Pluto, it will be one of the most productive and challenging periods of your life, but if the energy internalises it can be destructive and debilitating. I know a Scorpio woman who decided to use the transforming power of Pluto to transform herself. As Pluto moved through her Sun sign, she scheduled extensive plastic surgery. The operation was a success and the result is stunning.

Your health and Pluto/Sun sign activation

The health factors mentioned above — the reproductive, eliminative and defence systems, require additional nutrients and protective measures during Pluto/Sun sign activation. There can be strain on the heart and back and certain individuals may place themselves at risk by becoming involved in hazardous situations or by over-extending their energy reserves. Allergies are common. Eileen Nauman suggests that severe vitamin and mineral deficiencies are possible with the Pluto/Sun combination.

Chapter Ten

Personal Multi-Cycles and World Health Cycles

PERSONAL MULTI-CYCLES

There are key periods in our life when more than one planetary cycle or sub-cycle will operate simultaneously. Depending upon our age, circumstances and constitution, these periods can prove to be a physical and emotional trial. The planetary influences are extremely variable and the more influences operating simultaneously, the more our minds and bodies will have to adapt.

In summarising the biological correspondences of certain slow-moving planets described in previous chapters, it should be borne in mind that Jupiter denotes enlargement, growth and expansion; Saturn denotes hardening, ageing, stiffening, blocking; Uranus denotes erratic, unsettling, unexpected conditions; Neptune denotes a weakening and slackness of function, hypersensitivity, mystery ailments, lowered resistance and infection.

Relevant personal multi-cycles

The following are relevant life periods when multi-cycles and sub-cycles operate. A complete cycle is the return of a planet to its birth position; a sub-cycle is a significant period within the cycle.

20 to 21 years of age

The combined influence of Saturn, Uranus and Neptune is often experienced as a desire to break new ground or 'break away', as tension through responsibility, inner and outer changes. Security, or lack of it, becomes an issue. But the individual is usually quite physically resilient at this age.

29 to 30 years of age

Saturn, Jupiter and a recurrence of the natal lunar phase by progression, combine to generate positive thought processes following a period of contemplation and reassessment. There is often a breakthrough after a physical test, self-realisation following confusion, the desire to be true to oneself and a need to pay the price of progress.

42 to 45 years of age — the 'mid-life crisis'

Significant sub-cycles of Jupiter, Saturn, Uranus and Neptune are in operation. The sheer quantity of cycles adds to the complexity of this life period. Combined with the ageing, stiffening influence of Saturn, there is the rebellious, tense influence of Uranus, the over-expectation and a desire to expand which is associated with Jupiter, and finally the hypersensitivity of Neptune. Such a combination suggests dissatisfaction with existing circumstances leading to a search for a new direction, physical and chemical imbalance, physical conditions stemming from emotional difficulties, rebelling against the inevitable, a loss of perspective.

Most people between the ages of 42 and 45 years are at the peak of their working life and under extraordinary pressure. It is not uncommon for a sudden illness to manifest as a direct result of over-extending oneself, especially if the individual does not have the added strength and support of a healthy diet and lifestyle.

Close to 45 years of age, there is a tendency for both the positive and negative physical and personality traits to be magnified. In addition, the sensitive health factors indicated in the birth horoscope will be magnified and tested at this time. A great rise or fall is common during the mid-forties, so the health must be carefully monitored and positive preventive action taken. Those who have a strong constitution and good health indicators in the birth horoscope will find that their personal strengths are reinforced at this time.

The period between 42 and 45 is often a time of 'confronting the karma' — a type of spiritual recognition which can initiate action beyond the realms of common sense and logic. It can prove to be an unnerving and debilitating period if the spiritual self is denied and the call of duty uncompromisingly adhered to. A general re-focus and re-evaluation of perspectives is common and this can lead to an improved lifestyle and a more philosophical attitude. Many people direct their energies into readjusting their career and relationships to suit their new approach; others develop their talents, hobbies and recreational pursuits. The ultimate expression of the mid-life crisis is to expand and consolidate the personal potential.

59 to 63 years of age

Jupiter, Saturn, Uranus and Neptune are once again highlighted, but this time in different sub-cycles to the 42-45 years period. There is a second recurrence of the natal lunar phase by progression, the first having occurred at 29-30 years. Change is less comfortable at this time of life, but it is still important for new seeds to be planted. New interests will generate new and lasting friendships. The pressure areas of the body are highlighted and illnesses will fluctuate in intensity or present intermittently. A regular blood-pressure check is advisable. Some form of mild exercise could benefit the heart and blood flow. If necessary, make sensible dietary adjustments in order to minimise risk.

82 to 84 years of age

During this period the influences of Uranus and Neptune are in operation. It is a physically and emotionally vulnerable period when relationships may not live up to expectations. Many people choose to withdraw and live in seclusion. Development of the higher spiritual self is as important as maintaining interests and social contacts. Do not take the easy way out and slip into the dream state of nostalgia. Whilst the Neptune influence generates sensitivity, the approach of the Uranus return will generate a self-willed and radical approach to others, which may not be compatible with the situation in which the person finds himself or herself. Endeavour to utilise the Uranus energy to protect your personal rights.

The determination will increase at 84 years of age, when positive changes are still possible. The spirit of adventure will return at this point, or soon after. I have heard of several cases of 84-year-olds commencing new and exciting lifestyles in different surroundings.

WORLD HEALTH CYCLES

The study of planetary cycles and their relationship to world history is a fascinating research topic. The variable orbital speeds of the planets means that they will align or form conjunctions in the heavens at specific intervals. The faster moving planet overtakes, completes another revolution through the solar system and eventually catches up to the same slow-moving planet years later, to form another conjunction and commence a new cycle. There are many cycles open to research, depending upon your area of interest. The 20-year cycle of Jupiter and Saturn and the 45-year cycle of Saturn and Uranus, are indicative of world financial and political trends. The 36-year Saturn and Neptune cycle is also indicative of political trends, but the Saturn/Neptune cycles are major signicators of world health trends.

The Plague

This contagious epidemic disease is caused by the germ known as *Pasteurella pestis,* which was not identified until 1894 when Shibasaburo Kitasato and Alexandre Yersin discovered it quite independently of each other. The bacterium is passed to a person by fleas from infected rats. (The Sylvatic plague was carried by other rodents such as squirrels, rabbits and chipmunks.)

- The deadly Bubonic Plague, otherwise known as the Black Plague or Black Death, could be spread from person to person by droplet spray. It was named the 'Black Death' because of the black haemorrhages suffered by those afflicted by the illness.
- The first record of the plague in Europe was in Athens in 430 BC. One of the worst plagues, in Rome in AD 262, is said to have killed 5,000 people a day.
- The most widespread plague began in Constantinople in 1334 and it is believed the returning Crusaders were an important factor in the spread of this disease. It continued for nearly twenty years and wiped out a large percentage of the population of Europe and Asia as it spread through China, India, Persia, Russia, Italy, France, England, Germany and Norway.
- In 1665 London was in the grip of the Great Plague, which killed over 150,000 people. William Lilly (1602-1681) was an English astrologer who specialised in horary and predictive astrology. Lilly achieved fame and notoriety when he predicted the Great Plague of London and the Great Fire of London in 1666. Astrologers who make such precise predictions are

usually endowed with a marked psychic ability. Lilly was born on 1 May, 1602. See Chapter 14, for Lilly's birth horoscope.

The Great Fire of London started in a baker's shop in Pudding Lane on 2 September, 1666 and raged out of control for five days. It virtually destroyed the city, wiping out St Paul's Cathedral, over 80 other churches, the Royal Exchange, many public buildings and about 13,000 homes. By some miracle, no reported deaths occurred. The Great Fire had caused huge financial losses, but it had sterilised the city. The people were forced to call upon their deepest inner resources to rebuild their city and their lives.

Figure 8 is a horoscope for the commencement of the Great Fire, calculated for London at 12 noon on 2 September, 1666. It outlines the prevailing astrological conditions in London on the day. The Sun was in Virgo and the Moon was in Libra but moved into Scorpio that evening. Mars in Scorpio was sextile to Saturn and sesquiquadrate to Pluto, a pattern of frustrated violence. The most outstanding feature is the approaching conjunction of Saturn and Neptune. With Saturn at 14 degrees 0 minutes Capricorn and Neptune at 19 degrees 38 minutes Capricorn, the effects of the conjunction were striking. The exact conjunction occurred in January 1667, but in a 36-year cycle, a few months is not a great time span. Significant events often coincide with the period immediately prior to a major conjunction. At the time of the fire Pluto was conjunction to the Moon nodes (= a mass destiny, the intervention of a high power). Jupiter was square to Pluto (= make or lose a million, the reassessment of values and priorities) and Venus was square to Saturn (= sad losses, economy, separations).

In addition, I calculated a chart for 1 June, 1665, when the Great Plague was at its peak. Saturn was already in Capricorn at 7 degrees 35 minutes and Neptune was at 19 degrees 34 minutes of Capricorn. It is interesting that the 1989 conjunctions of Saturn and Neptune were also in Capricorn. The AIDS epidemic was gaining momentum in the years prior to the conjunctions.

The Saturn/Neptune conjunctions ... an astrological viewpoint
The conjunctions have a remarkable effect upon humanity in that they generate a reversion to basic principles. Materially they

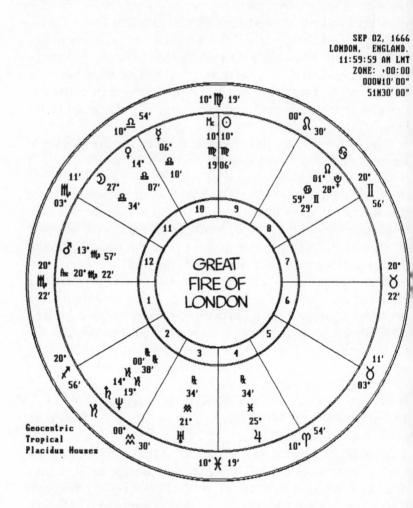

Figure 8: *The Great Fire of London*

are usually associated with hard times, but spiritually and artistically they herald new growth. Reinhold Ebertin interprets the combination of Saturn and Neptune as 'a struggle between idealistic and materialistic tendencies'. But I believe they also present to us an opportunity to ground our ideals and inspirations and make them real, because at the time of the conjunctions life's charades are erased and we become acutely aware of our true values.

Saturn and Neptune do not sit comfortably together. Saturn is formative, crystallising, conservative and wise, whilst Neptune is compassionate, intangible, sensitive and without boundaries. Negatively combined, they guarantee that the material things in life become intangible and out of reach. Positively combined we experience a heightened perception and take greater responsibility for the welfare of the less fortunate. Actions based on fear and psychic awareness produce remarkable good.

The conjunctions of Saturn and Neptune frequently coincide with a world health crisis. It is difficult to link a conjunction with a twenty year plague, but Saturn was conjunction to Neptune in 1344, the midway point of the European/Asian plague, which commenced in 1334.

In earlier conjunctions, such as the Great Plague and Great Fire of London, it seemed that Nature, people or an act of God intervened, but in more recent conjunctions, because of advanced technology and through sheer necessity, medical science progressed at an accelerated rate. In recent times when Saturn and Neptune slowly move towards their conjunctions, world health conflicts surface, and a huge concentration of energy and resources are directed into devising cures.

Some interesting examples are as follows:–

• 1846 — Saturn conjunction, Neptune in Aquarius
  In 1846 ether anaesthesia, administered by William Morton, was first demonstrated publicly in Massachusetts, USA.

• 1882 — Saturn conjunction, Neptune in Taurus
  In 1894 the plague reappeared in Hong Kong and ships from Hong Kong spread the plague around the world. India suffered most and more than 10,000,000 people died from the plague between 1894 and 1914.

• August 1917 — Saturn conjunction, Neptune in Leo

In 1918 a worldwide influenza epidemic killed millions.

In the late 1800s Louis Pasteur established the existence of living microbes which were associated with specific diseases. He observed that one micro-organism could destroy another, which he theorised could halt the spread of disease.

In London in 1928 Sir Alexander Fleming observed that *Penicillium notatum,* a common mould, could destroy staphyloccoccus in culture. But a practical method of extracting the penicillin was not devised until 1938.

In 1935 Gerhard Domagk, a German doctor, developed sulfa drugs to kill infection in animals. The drugs were later developed to treat humans.

- November 1952 and May/July 1953 — Saturn conjunction, Neptune in Libra.

The polio epidemic was pronounced. In 1953 Dr Jonas Salk, an American research scientist, developed a polio vaccine. Dr Salk and his family were among the first to receive the vaccine; in 1954 it was mass-tested and by 1955 was in general use.

- March, June and November 1989 — Saturn conjunction Neptune in Capricorn.

As mentioned above, the conjunctions were also in Capricorn at the time of the Great Plague in London. The AIDS epidemic, which came to the notice of the world in 1981, reached a crescendo in 1989. With the rapid increase in the number of cases, AIDS research accelerated and in June 1989 Dr Jonas Salk unveiled an experimental drug which he claimed had cured chimpanzees infected with AIDS. Although further research was required, Dr Salk had high hopes of developing a vaccine to prevent AIDS infection in humans and cure those already infected. At the time of his announcement the drug had already been tried on humans and had been well-tolerated.

It is fascinating that the same Dr Salk who did so much for humanity in 1953 with his polio vaccine, once again attempted to pioneer new horizons in medical science when Saturn and Neptune were again conjunction in 1989. Dr Salk is a Scorpio, born on 28 October, 1914, and his horoscope is described in Chapter 14.

Cause or effect?

We can hardly presume that the Saturn/Neptune cycles themselves could create worldwide epidemics, but I like to think of them as reminders to humanity, symbolic indicators that our house is not in order. The years leading up to the conjunction represent a clouding of awareness and values. The conjunctions shake us from our lethargy into a phase of increasing light and new perspectives.

This can best be illustrated by the other major factor of 1989, the worldwide recognition of the greenhouse effect and the willingness of the people to participate in the preservation of our planet. The fear, psychic awareness and responsibility associated with Saturn/Neptune, which I spoke of earlier, bonded together to produce ultimate good for all. The year 1989 was a year in which self-interest in diet and health was heavily promoted. Fibre, cellulite and anti-smoking were big news as more people discovered that they need not accept illness as a natural course of life.

FUTURE WORLD HEALTH PATTERNS

The next conjunction of Saturn and Neptune is in the early degrees of Aries in February 2026, although the two planets are closely aligned during most of 2025. It is difficult to predict what effect the next conjunction will have upon our planet when the full repercussions of the 1989 conjunctions have not been realised at the time of writing this book. But as we know, the sign of Aries means independence and the pioneering spirit. Perhaps there will be a further progression towards personal responsibility for health and welfare.

During 2025, the lead-up year to the conjunction, the focus will centre on poisons, medicines, pollution, personal and political immunity, martyrdom, the oceans and their harvest, water farming, accommodation on water, clean drinking water and new ways of achieving it. Many of the problems which exist now will not be completely resolved by then, or alternatively there may be a different set of problems resulting from the resolution of the 1989 problems. The year 2026 may well be a year of enforcement of laws to protect the whole rather than specific individuals. But as in the past it will be a vulnerable period for world health, which will test the most brilliant minds of the time.

Those born in the years of the conjunctions

Naturally the conjunctions will appear in the horoscopes of all those born in conjunction years. They act as a generation factor, involving shared experiences and attitudes of the times. The babies born in 1989 will carry into life with them the re-awakening of world awareness to certain values concerning our environment and relationships, as a result of past ecological abuse and promiscuity.

Will those born in conjunction years be more prone to illness than others? Not necessarily. Much depends on the date, time of birth and place of birth as to whether the conjunction will be strategically placed in the birth chart. Every birth horoscope has its vulnerable areas, but the Saturn/Neptune conjunction can be especially vulnerable if aspecting the Sun, Moon, Ascendant or Midheaven (the personal points).

Peter and Barry were both born in 1953, when Saturn and Neptune were in conjunction in Libra. Although Libra rules the kidneys, do not assume that all those born in 1953 will develop a kidney weakness. But in this case, both suffered from kidney ailments.

Peter is one of the successful kidney-transplant patients discussed in Chapter 12. He was born on 17 September, 1953 in Belgium. The Saturn/Neptune conjunction was not in hard aspect to the Sun, Moon, Ascendant or Midheaven in his birth horoscope, although it was square to Uranus. There were aspects to the conjunction, but they were generally favourable.

Barry was born on 21 August, 1953 in New South Wales, Australia, less than a month before Peter. His kidney disease was the result of an infection suffered in his early twenties. He never received a transplant, although his kidneys stopped functioning and he was on dialysis for some time. When Barry was born, Venus was conjunction to Uranus in Cancer and both were square to the Saturn/Neptune conjunction. The Venus/Uranus/Saturn/Neptune planetary combination was linked to the Ascendant and Midheaven by 45-degree and 135-degree aspects. In other words, Barry was extremely susceptible. By the time Peter was born a month later, Venus had moved into Leo.

As a creative and dynamic Leo, Barry was a brilliant innovator with a desire to live life to the full. When he became ill he refused to accept his limitations and modify his lifestyle. He died at the age of 27.

Venus/Uranus and Saturn/Neptune are two of the six recurring planetary patterns tabled in my research of 102 cases of kidney disease (Chapter 12). The particular Saturn/Neptune conjunction effecting Peter and Barry occurred in July 1953. When both men were born the conjunction had already occurred and the planets were separating. When Barry was born in August, Saturn and Neptune were only 1.5 degrees apart. By the time Peter was born in September they were nearly 3.5 degrees apart and rapidly becoming less effective.

Chapter Eleven

Periods of Lowered Resistance and Personal Depletion Factors

PERIODS OF LOWERED RESISTANCE

Each sign of the zodiac has specific areas of vulnerability. (Chapter 3 examines the body areas of each sign.) Although periods of lowered resistance can occur under a variety of astrological conditions, the full birth horoscope is required to accurately assess the strengths and weaknesses inherent in the make-up of each individual. But important information can still be gleaned from the Sun sign alone.

Ensure that you are familiar with your opposite sign. The opposite polarities are as follows: –

Aries is opposite to Libra
Taurus is opposite to Scorpio
Gemini is opposite to Sagittarius
Cancer is opposite to Capricorn
Leo is opposite to Aquarius
Virgo is opposite to Pisces.

In addition to your own sign, check out the body areas for your opposite sign and treat them with tender loving care. It is common to become depleted in the body areas of your opposite sign. The cell salts, helpful herbs and foods for your opposite sign may be useful supplements for you.

If you have had your full horoscope calculated, take particular notice of your Ascendant sign and Moon sign and once again refer to Chapter 3 for the body areas. The Ascendant sign represents your physical body, so it is of vital importance when assessing the health; the Moon sign will provide information concerning your emotions and body fluids.

The sign in which Mars is placed at birth is also significant. The body areas represented by the Mars sign may be susceptible to inflammations and accidents. For example, if Mars (inflammation) is placed in Taurus (the throat) at birth, the person would be susceptible to sore throats when tired or run down. Your Mars sign can also represent an area of personal power and energy. Individuals with Mars in Taurus can often generate great power through their throat and voice. The great Australian opera singer Joan Sutherland, who was born under the Sun sign of Scorpio, has Mars rising in Taurus. But there is no doubt that Joan would occasionally suffer from an inflamed throat.

Saturn takes 2.5 years to move through each zodiac sign. Even if you have not had your horoscope calculated you can assess the sign Saturn was in when you were born by referring to the dates listed under the Saturn cycles of health (Chapter 7). Your Saturn sign indicates a sluggish body area.

The following are suggestions as to when additional measures can be taken to guarantee continued good health and well-being.

The month prior to your birthday

The month prior to your birthday is frequently a period of lowered resistance. As cycles go, it is the period immediately preceding the commencement of your new solar year, which represents a lull in the physical life force. Ideally, it is a period of spiritual growth, to cleanse and prepare you for the year ahead. For more information on this period see the section covering solar return in Chapter 6.

Planetary activation of the Sun sign

The current placement of the slow-moving planets Jupiter, Saturn, Uranus, Neptune and Pluto in relation to your Sun sign can indicate periods of lowered resistance, especially if any of these planets are currently placed in your sign or your opposite sign. The chapters on cycles of health give the placements of these planets in the zodiac signs.

Quincunx activation of the Sun sign

The periods in your life when the slow-moving planets Saturn and Neptune move through your Quincunx or Inconjunct signs can coincide with periods of lowered resistance, that is ...

ARIES people may experience lowered resistance when Saturn or Neptune move through Virgo and Scorpio.
TAURUS people when Saturn or Neptune move through Libra

and Sagittarius.

GEMINI people when Saturn or Neptune move through Scorpio and Capricorn.

CANCER people when Saturn or Neptune move through Sagittarius and Aquarius.

LEO people when Saturn or Neptune move through Capricorn and Pisces.

VIRGO people when Saturn or Neptune move through Aquarius and Aries.

LIBRA people when Saturn or Neptune move through Pisces and Taurus.

SCORPIO people when Saturn or Neptune move through Aries and Gemini.

SAGITTARIUS people when Saturn or Neptune move through Taurus and Cancer.

CAPRICORN people when Saturn or Neptune move through Gemini and Leo.

AQUARIUS people when Saturn or Neptune move through Cancer and Virgo.

PISCES people when Saturn or Neptune move through Leo and Libra.

The chapters on cycles of health give the placements of Saturn and Neptune in the zodiac signs. The Quincunx signs are covered more fully in Chapter 4.

Planetary cycles
Complete cycles and semi-cycles of Jupiter, Saturn, Uranus, Neptune and Pluto occur at specific ages in life. They often coincide with crisis situations and major life changes, which in turn can lead to periods of lowered resistance. Our inner spiritual quality will determine how we deal with life tests, and whether or not a crisis will manifest as an illness.

Your secondary progressed Sun sign
The secondary progressed horoscope provides further information as to vulnerable body areas during the life. Secondary progression is an astrological technique used by the experienced astrologer. It is an ancient technique, representing the unfold-

ing and development of our life through its various phases and employs the symbolic representation of 'one day for every year of life'. Reference to this symbolism can be found in the Bible in the Book of Ezekiel (Chapter 4: 4,5).

The twelve signs of the zodiac rise and set every twenty-four hours as the Earth rotates. The great annual journey of the Earth through the heavens places the Sun in each of the twelve zodiac signs of the tropical zodiac during a twelve month period. The ancients symbolically equated the twenty-four hours to twelve months.

Those of you who think of yourselves only in terms of your Sun sign will be interested to learn that everyone over thirty years of age will have experienced some of the characteristics of the zodiac sign following their own. Naturally we retain the characteristics of our birth sign, but time and maturity modifies our attitudes. For the layperson, it will suffice to say that secondary directions are based on the days immediately following the date of birth; these days are symbolic of the years of life after birth. In other words, twenty-one days after your birthday is equivalent to your twenty-first year of life, which means that during your lifetime your Sun sign will progress through two or three zodiac signs following your own, depending on how long you live. For example a person born with the Sun in Libra will progress through Scorpio and Sagittarius during their lifetime. The zodiac signs are always placed in the same sequence, and are listed many times in this book. Individuals who progress through Pisces, the twelfth sign of the zodiac, will then progress to Aries, the first sign of the zodiac.

As you progress through the zodiac signs following your own, you will be more prone to the illnesses affecting these signs. The changeover years from one sign to the next will vary from individual to individual, and will depend entirely upon your exact date of birth.

The balsamic factor

The secondary progressed horoscope is an excellent indicator of current and future health trends in the individual. A common factor to people born under all signs is the 3.5 year period between the secondary progressed balsamic Moon phase and

some potential for a depletion of iron and Vitamin B_{12} during Mars activation.

Taurus (ruled by Venus)
Cell salt: Natrum Sulphuretum (Nat Sulph)
The function of Nat Sulph is to eliminate excess water and aid the digestive process.

Helpful herbs: Mint, thyme and dandelion to assist the digestive function. Raspberry leaves and lovage infusions will soothe sore throats.

Fruit, especially berry fruit such as blackberries and blueberries, iodine foods such as seafood or kelp for the thyroid gland and beetroot for the liver, are useful dietary supplements for Taureans. Avoid foods which are high in sugar and starch.

Physical affection and creative outlets are important prerequisites for the well-being of the Taurean. As an Earth sign, Taurus can benefit from working in the garden and participating in outdoor activities. Cravings for specific foods should be carefully examined to determine whether there is an unfulfilled emotional need.

Venus activation relates to the glands and hormones, kidneys, veins, lovemaking and fertility. Foods high in Vitamin E will stimulate and help prevent malfunction in these areas. Venus transits generate an urge to indulge, beautify and create.

Gemini (ruled by Mercury)
Cell salt: Kali Muriaticum (Kali Mur)
Kali Mur forms fibrin and helps prevent congestion in the bronchial tubes.

Helpful herbs: Parsley for nutrition, kidneys and digestion, horseradish and mulberries for coughs and colds and lavender, sage and valerian for the nerves.

Geminis thrive on foods which are rich in natural vitamins and minerals, such as alfalfa, bean shoots, tomatoes, pineapple, figs and mushrooms.

Geminis have a high output of nervous energy, which can result in nutritional depletion and sleeplessness. They need plenty of sleep and fresh air and will notice a marked improvement in their health if they join a reputable yoga school. Yoga improves the nerves, lungs and general outlook.

Alice Portman believes that many Geminis require vitamin supplements to counteract deficiencies created by overstrain and smoking and suggests vitamins B and C.

Mercury activation heightens nervous reaction, but can also quicken the personal pace. Writing, correspondence and all communications will be approached with added enthusiasm. Personal mobility increases and sometimes a trip is planned. An increase in the B group of vitamins, either as supplements, or through foods rich in the B group, is recommended during Mercury activation.

Cancer (ruled by the Moon)
Cell salt: Calcareum Fluoricum (Cal Fluor)
Cal Fluor has a toning and elasticising quality. Cancerians have a sensitive nature, which can sometimes have a detrimental effect on their self-confidence; Cal Fluor will strengthen the Cancerian courage.

Helpful herbs: Balm for the reproductive system, agrimony for diarrhoea and arrowroot to relax the stomach.

Foods to aid the digestion and absorption of nutrients are important to the Cancerian. If it can be satisfactorily tolerated, warm milk, honey and raisins are soothing supplements. Eat plenty of fruit and vegetables which have an abundance of natural iron. Lettuce has relaxing and cooling properties. Cucumber is a good potassium food. Like all of the water signs, Cancerians will benefit from oil baths, massage and periods spent by the sea or near lakes.

Moon activation plays on the emotions and liquid balance in the body. People born under the sign of Cancer are extremely aware of the Moon phases on the subconscious level. Mark the dates of the new Moon and the full Moon on your calendar. Regulate your attitudes and endeavour to be flexible at these times.

Eileen Nauman maintains that the correct balance of riboflavin (Vitamin B_2) and potassium will help counteract the symptoms of irritability and water retention.

Leo (ruled by the Sun)
Cell salt: Magnesium Phosphoricum (Mag Phos)
Mag Phos acts on the motor nerves, relieving pain, strain, cramp

and stress. Leo is a dynamic sign and consequently many Leos over-extend themselves, both mentally and physically. Mag Phos should not be used as a substitute for adequate rest and care, but can assist in the relaxation process.

Helpful herbs: The ever-popular chamomile tea, sweetened with honey, is a special treat for the world-weary Leo at the end of a busy day. Borage is said to benefit the heart and circulation and saffron to ease palpitations.

As a Fire sign, the Leo is often attracted to 'heavy fuel' nutrients such as red meat. Because Leos are susceptible to heart conditions and cholesterol-related disorders, they are advised to choose lean red meat and limit the quantity consumed. Fish and skinless chicken make excellent substitutes. Eggs, nuts, raisins, coconut, cabbage, oranges and peaches are beneficial foods for Leos.

Leos thrive on love, attention and enjoying life, so that personal expression is important to them. They should be encouraged to become involved in creative outlets such as music, dance and theatre.

Sun activation relates to personal strength and spiritual regeneration. It emanates warmth, positivity and ego-consciousness. Eileen Nauman links vitamins A and D and magnesium to the Sun. She states: 'To have a strong, pulsing life force — the heart — we need sufficient Vitamin A.'

Virgo (ruled by Mercury)
Cell salt: Kali Sulphuricum (Kali sulph)
The function of Kali Sulph is to lubricate, purify and ventilate the body — qualities especially helpful to Virgos, who are susceptible to disorders of the lower digestive tract and bowels. Kali Sulph is beneficial for skin and hair disorders.

Helpful herbs: Mint and fennel to assist the digestion, dandelion for the liver and valerian to calm the nerves. Natural foods are best for Virgos, who thrive on apples, celery, beetroot and lemons. Digestive problems could stem from poor absorption of food or congestion of the liver. Sprouted seeds such as alfalfa and fenugreek will help maintain inner harmony and ease internal inflammations. Alice Portman recommends slippery elm and grain foods (preferably millet) as suitable natural remedies for Virgos.

Many Virgos worry unnecessarily. Meditation will help them to relax and channel their thought patterns into the constructive outlets necessary to ensure their future success and happiness.

Mercury activation steps up nervous reactions. In the case of Virgos, the stomach can be affected as a result of over-commitment and worry and physical activities are important at this time, in order to create a sense of balance. As mentioned in the Mercury activation of Gemini, an increase in the B group of vitamins, either as foods or supplements, is recommended during Mercury activation.

Libra (ruled by Venus)
Cell salt: Natrum Phosphase (Nat Phos)
Nat Phos maintains the correct water balance and acid/alkaline balance in the body. Librans who enjoy an inner balance are more likely to be happier and healthier in their everyday life.

Helpful herbs: Dandelion is a good general tonic — it is a diuretic and is valuable for liver and kidney disorders. Thyme is helpful for headaches and giddiness. Parsley is well-known for its nutritional qualities; fresh parsley should be eaten regularly in salads or sprinkled on other foods.

Lemon juice in warm water, taken upon awakening, will stimulate and cleanse the kidneys. Alice Portman recommends almonds and pineapple as nutritional foods for Librans, the majority of whom take a special interest in their appearance, especially their hair and skin.

Venus activation relates to the glands and hormones, kidneys, veins, lovemaking and fertility. Foods high in Vitamin E will stimulate and help prevent malfunction in these areas. Venus transits generate an urge to indulge, beautify and create.

Scorpio (ruled by Pluto)
Cell salt: Calcium Sulphase (Calc Sulph)
The function of Calc Sulph is to protect, heal and purify. Cal Sulph assists in the prevention of ulceration and the accumulation of pus and expedites the healing of skin disorders and eruptions. The sign of Scorpio is associated with the repro-

ductive, eliminative and defence systems; Calc Sulph will lesson the tendency towards infection in these areas.

Helpful herbs: Basil for its healing qualities, blackcurrant for throat and other inflammations, garlic the cleanser, chicory and olive the laxatives and Ginseng the stimulant.

The Scorpio way is to purge and cleanse. Emotional blockages can be cleared and life difficulties recognised by unblocking and unlocking, that is by eliminating the wastes from the physical body.

Scorpios will improve their sense of well-being if they include plenty of fruit and vegetables in their diet. Onions, cabbage, oranges, lemons, rhubarb and prunes are beneficial foods for Scorpios.

Pluto activation is associated with imbalances in the body which can be either emotional or physical. Pluto brings subconscious feelings to the surface, where they must be acknowledged and dealt with if physical illness is to be avoided. Pluto activation can also generate allergic reactions. The keywords for Pluto activation are 'intensity' and 'transformation'. Alice Portman has found that Pluto activation can lead to a depletion of zinc. She suggests supplements of zinc foods such as oysters, sunflower and pumpkin seeds, during Pluto transits.

Sagittarius (ruled by Jupiter)
Cell salt: Silica
Silica assists the body in the control of infection and pus. It can add lustre to the hair and is associated with the teeth, nails, skin and sweat glands. Silica can be helpful for those who perspire excessively.

Helpful herbs: Sage for wisdom, courage and to aid digestion, dandelion and chicory for the liver and chervil as a diuretic and blood cleanser.

Grains will strengthen the Sagittarian constitution, in particular oats, oat bran and barley should be included in the diet. Other Sagittarian foods are apples, onions, asparagus, beetroot, cherries and prunes.

Jupiter activation generates exaggerated situations. Weight problems, cholesterol build-up and disorders of blood, liver and lungs are common manifestations of Jupiter activation. The intake of rich, acidic foods should be limited and physical exercise and outdoor activities increased. As Jupiter rules the body fats, the inclusion of lecithin in the diet during Jupiter activation may help to prevent an accumulation of fats.

Capricorn (ruled by Saturn)
Cell salt: Calcium Phosphase (Calc Phos)

Calc Phos is found in the bones, teeth, blood, connective tissue and gastric juices. It assists in the absorption of calcium, so is essential for young, growing bodies, menopausal women and the elderly. It aids in the healing of bone fractures. Sufficient Cal Phos in the digestive juices prevents indigestion and the malabsorption of food.

Helpful herbs: Comfrey for coughs and colds and bone fractures, sorrel for sick headaches and blood cleansing, cloves for toothache and mustard for joint pains.

Capricorns need to sustain a satisfactory intake of calcium. Yoghurt is particularly suitable; in addition to a high calcium content, it is full of beneficial digestive stimulants. Beetroot is an excellent food for the liver and can be eaten cooked, grated in salads or taken as juice. Berry fruits, oranges, grapefruit and lemons are good skin foods. Capricorns should drink plenty of fresh water; this will flush toxins from the body and keep the skin clear.

Saturn activation can result in sluggishness and depression, but expressed positively, it can give one a sense of purpose and direction. There may be a depletion of minerals in the body. Foods and supplements which are rich in calcium, magnesium, vitamins C and D, will prove beneficial. Some effort should be made to motivate the body through exercise, which will step up the circulation and help the depression to lift. Capricorns should avoid isolating themselves from others.

Aquarius (ruled by Uranus)
Cell salt: Natrum Muriaticum (Nat Mur)

Nat Mur regulates the distribution of moisture in the body; an imbalance of water in the body can lead to headaches, constipation, watery secretions, excess mucus, sleeplessness or alternatively drowsiness, depending upon whether the balance is too dry or too moist. It is not surprising that Nat Mur is assigned to Aquarius; Aquarius is symbolised by a water carrier and rules the circulatory system. A craving for common salt suggests a deficiency of Nat Mur. As common salt is a contributing factor to hardened arteries and skin complaints, natural salt sources such as seafoods, sea vegetables and vegetable salt are preferable.

Helpful herbs: Elderberry for the nerves, rosemary for the heart, blood pressure and nervous headaches, and barley for nutrition, cramps, hair and nails. The high magnesium content in barley is excellent for the majority of Aquarians. Magnesium is attributed to the opposite sign of Leo, suggesting a potential depletion in the sign of Aquarius. Aquarians are thinking gourmets, who can work wonders with natural food combinations. They are mentally and physically at their best with foods which will not clog up their system. Carrots, celery, spinach, grapes and lemons, preferably eaten raw, are valuable Aquarian nutrients.

Uranus activation can generate changeable and erratic behaviour in those affected by its electrical energy. Alice Portman suggests a physical earthing by walking barefoot in the park or on garden soil. In winter, pure woollen socks and woollen fabric wrapped around the body will help to diffuse excess electricity. Meditation and yoga will quieten hyper-mental activity.

Pisces — (ruled by Neptune)
Cell salt: Ferrum Phosphase (Ferr Phos)
Ferr Phos is the iron cell salt; its function is to oxygenate the blood and assist in the formation of red blood corpuscles. Ferr Phos can offer some relief for those suffering from fevers, inflammations, haemorrhages, palpitations, bronchitis, injuries, anaemia and depression.

Helpful herbs: Bilberries for coughs, colds, diarrhoea, eczema and to ease water retention. Rose hips, a natural source of vitamins C, A, B, E and P, are essential to the body's defence system in its fight against infection and general illness. Kelp provides iodine and iron.

Pisceans must be discriminating about their intake of foods, tablets and drugs as many experience difficulty in absorbing nutrients. It is common for the Piscean to have a chemical or acid/alkaline imbalance, which can effect immunity and state of mind. A high protein diet is recommended, but seafoods, chicken and vegetable protein are preferable to red meat. Pisceans should avoid alcohol or drink it in small quantities. Foods which are easily digested and high in natural iron, such as spinach, raisins, dates, almonds, apricots, lima beans and liver, will increase the strength and confidence.

Neptune activation. To maintain close contact with water Pisceans should make regular visits to the sea, or to lakes and rivers if they live inland. Plenty of water should be drunk and warm baths, supplemented with aromatic body oil, enjoyed. Pisceans should vent their creativity, develop their spirituality and spend time on physical, emotional and mental health.

Chapter Twelve

The Onset of Illness

If you become ill, do you consider yourself to be an 'innocent bystander', a victim of circumstances? If so, perhaps you should consider taking an active role in dealing with your illness. Naturally you may require professional medical advice and treatment, but it is not necessary for you to stand by, feeling helpless. From an astrological viewpoint, there are several factors to consider when assessing the onset of illness.

1. Firstly the natal or birth horoscope indicates the areas of personal vulnerability. This is unchangeable.
2. The activated horoscope indicates periods of lowered resistance and tests of strength. These cannot be changed but our approach towards them can.
3. Our lifestyle, exercise and nutrition programmes suggest how our minds and bodies will deal with these tests. These can be improved.
4. There is an inner spiritual quality, sometimes inborn, sometimes gained from our upbringing and life experiences, which will navigate the way we deal with serious illness and other traumas. This can be developed.

Cancer

One of the most inspiring books I have read on approaching serious illness and overcoming it, is *You Can Conquer Cancer* by Ian Gawler. Ian suffered from bone cancer, and after the removal of his right leg in January 1975 and the reappearance of the cancer in November 1975, he was told in March 1976 that he only had two weeks to live. He took control of his life and created what he called 'a healing environment' for his body. In a clear and concise manner, Ian's book outlines his philosophies and the methods he used to overcome his illness. In June 1978 he was declared free of active cancer.

Ian Gawler believes cancer is a 'disease of society and a disease of lifestyle' and that 'there is a close link between the function of our body and the function of our psyche'. His research on cancer, cancer patients and the period in their life when the disease developed was of special interest to me as an astrologer. Ian observed that cancer was frequently preceded by traumatic, life-changing events such as the death of a spouse or retirement from a busy career. The patient was 'unable to cope with the major challenge, particularly where it involved a fundamental change in their life'.

An astrologer assessing the astrological 'down' periods in the life will not know exactly how they will manifest. For example, the influence of Saturn activation, manifesting negatively, can range from merely feeling tired to a major separation, responsibility or illness. The linking of life traumas with illness is no surprise to me. In the nineteen years I have worked with astrology I have seen the 'trauma *or* illness' as well as the 'trauma *and* illness' manifestations at work in people's lives. The different manifestations depend on the person's basic physical/hereditary make-up plus his or her emotional/spiritual approach to life.

Eleonora Kimmel is one of the top astrologers in the United States. Her speciality is cosmobiology and she has been a major contributor to the field of astrological medical research. As Executive Director of *The Cosmobiology Journal* (now *Cosmobiology International*), Eleonora Kimmel published an essay by Dr Schwab, MD, in the February 1979 issue. Dr Schwab's essay was originally published in 1933 in *Kosmobiologie*, 45 Jahrgang 1978 and translated by Dr Karl R. Wagner of Miami, Florida USA. (Dr Schwab died soon after World War II ended.) His essay provided valuable guidelines in the research of cancer and its medical-astrological links.

Dr Schwab believed that 'cancer is a disease of the soul and the lymphatic nervous system in which life retreats from the organs'. He said that 'every human being possesses a predisposition towards cancer, carries its seeds.' He developed a profile of the person who is most likely to develop cancer …

> *1. People who overindulge their bodies with albumen (meat and eggs) hamper the permeation of the soul throughout the body (slowing down of the thymus gland).*
>
> *2. Those past their 40th year decrease their soul permeation.*

Life energy retreats from the organs if they do not train them-
selves to counteract that retreat.

3. People who lose control of their body through singular
application of their emotional and rational life to one partic-
ular aspect such as worry or unhappiness sacrifice the perme-
ation of the soul (destruction of the sympathetic).

4. People who live in a materialistic age which considers the
body a collection of matter and the organs as machines, create
a stranglehold on the sympathetic.

5. Those who allow a continuous irritation or abrasive influ-
ence to affect a specific organ will sustain a counter perme-
ation of the soul which has an adverse effect on the whole; in
such areas cancer can gain a foothold.'

Dr Schwab based his findings on 129 cases of cancer of the
stomach, 53 cases of abdominal cancer, 121 cases of breast
cancer and 126 cases of the esophagus.

Astrologically he concluded:

1. That a lack of Fire signs (Aries, Leo and Sagittarius) in the
   birth chart provided insufficient oxidation for the body. The
   person with such a birth chart must endeavour to develop the
   kundalini fire and oxygenate their body through yoga breathing and exercise. He suggests that people without Fire signs
   should surround themselves with all things and people under
   the influence of the Fire signs. I have already reached these
   conclusions (see Chapter 4, 'Too much or too little of the one
   element'), but I think of this attraction to the missing element
   as more of a natural sequence. People intuitively know what is
   good for them; they know what they lack and who can provide
   it.

2. An abundance of what he termed 'the signs of dense spiritual
   penetration', that is Pisces, Taurus and Libra, which he said
   can tolerate only limited amounts of albumen, will give a sus-
   ceptibility to cancer.

Dr Schwab also cited the sign of Libra, the late degrees of
Sagittarius and the early degrees of Capricorn, as recurring
Ascendant positions of cancer patients.

I believe that cancer may be more of a Yin illness than a Yang
illness. Those with a predominance of the Yin signs of Taurus,
Cancer, Virgo, Scorpio, Capricorn and Pisces in their horo-

scope, could be more susceptible to cancer and other illnesses of this nature, because of their tendency to internalise many of their deepest responses. The Yang signs of Aries, Gemini, Leo, Libra, Sagittarius and Aquarius, find it easier to shake off negativity because it is more natural for them to externalise, re-channel or re-orientate. However, Dr Schwab's Libra and Sagittarius findings do not conform: neither Libra or Sagittarius are Yin signs.

3. The placement and strength of influence of Venus and the Moon in the horoscope is significant. Dr Schwab pointed out that a disruptive relationship between Venus and the Moon 'results in the separation of the formative powers of the soul'. Remember that Venus rules the signs of Taurus and Libra; the Moon rules the sign of Cancer.

Other suggestions made by Dr Schwab for the prevention of cancer are to 'raise the conscious of all organs and all parts of the body'. He suggested additional attention to oxidation through specific cell salts, the intake of raw foods, fresh water and a satisfactory level of elimination of waste from the body.

Cancer case studies
The following four studies are from my own files. Certain personal details have been withheld to guarantee privacy for the persons involved.

1. Nancy was born in Victoria, Australia in 1954 with Sun, Mercury and Venus in Pisces, the Ascendant, Moon and Neptune in Libra and Capricorn on the Midheaven. She developed breast cancer at 33 years of age.

2. Dawn was born in Czechoslovakia in 1949 with the Sun and Mars in Pisces, Ascendant, Jupiter and Moon in Capricorn and Scorpio on the Midheaven. She developed cancer of the lymph nodes at 26 years of age.

3. Marianne was born in Germany in 1931 with the Sun in Sagittarius, Mars, Mercury, Venus, Moon and Saturn in Capricorn, Ascendant in Cancer and the Midheaven in Pisces. She developed breast cancer at 57 years of age.

4. Helene was born in the Netherlands in 1929 with the Sun in Capricorn, Moon and Jupiter in Taurus, the Ascendant in Cancer and Venus and the Midheaven in Pisces. She devel-

oped breast cancer at 56 years of age. Helene's detailed horoscope interpretation is included in Chapter 14.

Classification of Planetary Birth Positions — Cancer Cases

In order to make an initial assessment of the birth horoscope, we
apply a simple classification technique which can be used by
those with minimal knowledge of astrology, provided a complete
horoscope is available. It involves categorising the twelve positions of a birth chart into their different elements. (The elements and Yin and Yang categories have been described fully in
chapters 2 and 4.) As we assess each of the twelve positions, we
allocate additional weight to some planets and points, depending upon their significance and speed of orbit.

The Sun, Moon, Ascendant and Midheaven, which are known
as the 'personal points' are allocated 3 points each.

Mercury, Venus and Mars are allocated 2 points each.

Jupiter, Saturn, Uranus, Neptune and Pluto, the slow-moving
planets, are allocated 1 point each.

This technique is demonstrated, using Helene's chart as an
example. Her birth positions are as follows: –

Sun (3 points) in Capricorn (Earth) … 3 points to Earth.

Moon (3 points) in Taurus (Earth) … 3 points to Earth.

Ascendant (3 points) in Cancer (Water) … 3 points to Water.

Midheaven (3 points) in Pisces (Water) … 3 points to Water.

Mercury (2 points) in Aquarius (Air) … 2 points to Air.

Venus (2 points) in Pisces (Water) … 2 points to Water.

Mars (2 points) in Gemini (Air) … 2 points to Air.

Jupiter (1 point) in Taurus (Earth) … 1 point to Earth.

Saturn (1 point) in Sagittarius (Fire) … 1 point to Fire.

Uranus (1 point) in Aries (Fire) … 1 point to Fire.

Neptune (1 point) in Virgo (Earth) … 1 point to Earth.

Pluto (1 point) in Cancer (Water) … 1 point to Water.

In total, Helene has …

Fire 2 points, Earth 8 points, Air 4 points, Water 9 points.

Yin signs (Earth and Water) = 17 points.

Yang signs (Fire and Air) = 6 points.

The other three cancer patients have been classified into their
elements and Yin and Yang categories below: –

Nancy
Fire 3 points, Earth 0 points, Air 8 points, Water 12 points.
Yin signs 12 points, Yang signs 11 points.

Dawn
Fire 1 point, Earth 8 points, Air 6 points, Water 8 points.
Yin signs 16 points, Yang signs 7 points.

Marianne
Fire 5 points, Earth 11 points, Air 0 points, Water 7 points.
Yin signs 18 points, Yang signs 5 points.

Dawn, Marianne and Helene have an overload of Earth and Water, Nancy has an overload of Air and Water. Three of the four charts are low in the Fire element.

In the case of Nancy, with 8 points in Air, we must keep in mind that 7 of the 8 points can be attributed to the Ascendant, Moon and Neptune in Libra. Libra is one of Dr Schwab's signs of 'dense spiritual penetration' and the question of Libra's resilience in comparison to the other Air signs requires further research.

Kidney disease cases
Hereditary factors, infection and drugs are three of the causes of diseased and non-functioning kidneys. I have managed to collect a total of 102 cases of people with kidney disease, many of whom have had a kidney transplant, but only twenty-three of these have accurate birth data. Accurate birth data means that all twelve points of the horoscope are available for assessment.

These particular cases suggest that kidney disease may be more of a Yang illness than a Yin illness. There is a surprisingly high incidence of Fire signs in the group and many of the charts have an extreme imbalance of element placements. For example one person had 17 points in Fire, nil in Earth, nil in Air and 6 in Water; another had 7 points in Fire, 14 in Earth, 1 in Air and 1 in Water.

For general assessments only, the seventy-nine cases without a birth time can be included. For example, the distribution of Sun signs amongst the total 102 patients was as follows: –

Aries 11,	Taurus 10,	Gemini 8,
Cancer 9,	Leo 9,	Virgo 11,
Libra 7,	Scorpio 11,	Sagittarius 5,
Capricorn 7,	Aquarius 10,	Pisces 4.

In reviewing these figures it becomes obvious that the Sun sign alone does not provide enough information for an accurate assessment. Because Libra rules the kidneys, it should follow that there would be more people born under Libra suffering from kidney disease. However, this is not the case, although the opposite sign of Aries is strongly represented, which is significant. The opposite sign to your Sun sign does pinpoint an area of potential sensitivity.

Using only the Sun signs, the elements were found to be evenly distributed, which is contradictory to the smaller, more detailed study using accurate birth times. Amongst the Sun signs there were 25 Fire signs, 28 Earth signs, 25 Air signs and 24 Water signs.

The assessment of qualities showed a greater number of people born under the fixed Sun signs. The results of the assessment were: –

Cardinal (Aries, Cancer, Libra and Capricorn) 34
Fixed (Taurus, Leo, Scorpio and Aquarius) 40
Mutable (Gemini, Virgo, Sagittarius and Pisces) 28

The Planetary Connections (Aspects)

My total research disclosed a powerful and consistent correlation between certain planets and points. These points were: –

The Sun (general vitality)
Venus (the kidneys, glands)
Mars (inflammation)
Jupiter (organic systems, liver)
Saturn (blocking, restriction of function)
Uranus (anomaly of function)
Neptune (slackness of function).

The major planetary connections were between …

Sun and Neptune (weakened vitality, water concentrations in the cell)
Venus and Neptune (weakened glandular function)

Venus and Uranus (sudden anomaly in the function of glands)
Saturn and Neptune (undermining illness, illness with causes difficult to ascertain)
Mars and Neptune (point of infection)
Jupiter and Neptune (increase of water in the blood).
Of the group, 44 per cent had four or more of the planetary connections operating on their date of birth; 78 per cent had three or more of the planetary connections operating on their date of birth.

What is an Aspect?

An aspect (or planetary connection) is a mathematical relationship between two points in the horoscope. In the case of a natal horoscope, they occur at the moment of birth. There are many different aspects. For example two planets or points which are 90 degrees apart are said to be in 'square'. Without going into a long discussion on aspects, which you can find in any good astrology book, it will suffice to say that the relationships I used in the study were the conjunction (0 degrees), 30, 45, 60, 90, 120, 135, 150 and 180 degrees. Certain aspects, known as the 'harder, tense' aspects, were more apparent than the other aspects.

When comparing a number of cases of a specific type, in this case 102 people with kidney disease, it is important to compare them with an equal number of people without kidney disease (known as a control group). Because of the large quantity of horoscopes I process, this is not a difficult exercise. Meeting people off the street with a combination of four or more of the above planetary connections in a horoscope is certainly not a daily occurrence. (A good reference book for interpreting planetary combinations with emphasis on health is *The Combination of Stellar Influences* by Reinhold Ebertin, who during his lifetime, made an major contribution to astro-medical research.)

Kidney Transplants

In addition to the physical and legal implications of the transplant, there is also the spiritual implication. It is a well-known fact that living blood relatives make the best donars. Certain combinations of planetary patterns can recur in child, parent and grandparent or miss a generation and occur in grandparent and grandchild only (see Chapter 13).

But what of non-related donors and recipients of the organ? It would be interesting to compare the horoscope of a large number of donors and recipients of successful and unsuccessful transplants, in order to evaluate whether more compatible planetary patterns were operating in the successful transplant. Obtaining data for kidney recipients is not a problem, but unrelated donors are often young people who have died unexpectedly and to protect the families, their birth data is not readily available.

I have made a study of one successful transplant (Beverley) and one unsuccessful transplant (Graham). Beverley's donor was a living blood relative. Graham had two failed transplants, the first in 1976 from a cadaver (unknown) donor and the second in 1977 from a living blood relative.

The result of the study showed a dominant strength and vitality factor in Beverley's birth chart. Her mental attitude was stronger and more externalised than that of Graham, the unsuccessful transplant recipient.

Beverley, the successful recipient, had 5 points in Fire signs, 6 in Earth, 11 in Air and 1 in Water (or 7 Yin and 16 Yang).

Graham, the unsuccessful transplant recipient, had 7 points in Fire signs, 9 in Earth, nil in Air and 7 in Water (16 Yin and 7 Yang).

In Chapter 14, I have examined Graham's chart in relation to the date of his first unsuccessful kidney transplant in 1976 and commented on his second transplant.

The Organ lives on
When I was in Germany in 1973 I met Reinhold Ebertin for the first time. At that time he was 72 years old, with a lifetime of astrological experience at his disposal. His mother Elspeth Ebertin, had also been an astrologer. Through an interpreter I told Mr Ebertin of my research into kidney disease and he reminded me that although the kidney donor may die, a successful transplant means that the horoscope of the deceased person lives on and is to be compared with that of the recipient. As mentioned above I have not had the opportunity to conduct such an experiment due to the lack of accurate birth data of unrelated donors.

Transplant case

Peter's case was discussed earlier in Chapter 10, 'World Health Cycles'. He was born on 17 September, 1953 and had a very successful kidney transplant in 1973. The kidney donor was a deceased, unknown person. Peter is a Virgo with the Moon in Capricorn, a Scorpio Ascendant and Venus, Pluto and the Midheaven in Leo. One of Peter's most prominent traits is his determination, which is hardly surprising with Scorpio on the Ascendant. In total he has 6 points in Fire, 8 points in Earth, 5 points in Air and 4 points in Water signs (12 points in Yin signs; 11 points in Yang signs).

The obvious balance of the elements and Yin and Yang signs has been to Peter's advantage in his adjustment to this major change in his life. He tells me that in addition to his physical adjustment to the transplant, he underwent an important emotional and spiritual adjustment. He perceived himself differently and said the transplant changed him in ways he would not have expected of an operation. In his birth chart, Mercury, the planet of the mind, is in Libra, suggesting mental balance and adjustment through logical thought processes.

Peter's Midheaven (ego/identity) in Leo is conjunction to Venus (kidneys/glands, creativity) and Pluto (immunity, transformation), which would signify a creative transformation of identity through changes in glandular (kidney) function. The Moon (liquids in the body) in Capricorn forms an aspect to this pattern.

Timing the Operation

According to the rules of astrology, the time an operation is conducted makes a statement about its outcome. This includes emergency surgery; emergencies are just that, and the patient is hardly in a position to make any choices other than to pray and review the horoscope later. To plan an elective operation astrologically, the following could be taken into consideration: –

1. Avoid surgery on the full Moon; the full tide of the body at this time may cause haemorrhaging.
2. Avoid surgery on the new Moon. If other factors are favourable, the ideal time is five days before or after the new Moon.

3. In particular avoid surgery on eclipses of the Sun (which occur at certain new Moons) and eclipses of the Moon (which occur at certain full Moons).
4. Avoid surgery if the Sun or Moon is in the sign which rules the part of the body to be operated upon. In other words be cautious about commiting yourself to a throat operation if the Sun or Moon is in Taurus at the time of the operation.
5. An operation is a violent event for your body. Astrologically you can expect to see a violent energy pattern such as Mars and Uranus activating your chart at the time of the operation. A time chosen with a minimum of negative aspects is favoured. A badly placed Saturn can lead to a slow recuperation and the need for continuing treatment. A badly placed Neptune suggests a proneness to infection, the wrong diagnosis and drug allergies.
6. Rarely mentioned, but one factor which I feel is very important is the relationship between the doctor and patient. We have all heard of cases of brilliant doctors and naturopaths who have 'no luck' with certain patients. If the compatibility factor is strong, the positive energies between doctor and patient will enhance diagnosis and effective treatment. There is more involved in effective healing than science and textbooks and still much to be scientifically explained. For example, why does a life-threatening illness go into complete remission for some people and not others? Most people are intuitive; they are usually drawn to those who can help them and repelled by those who cannot. Unfortunately many do not trust their own intuition.

AIDS CASES

AIDS, the disease of the 1980s, was first reported in the United States in 1981. In January 1981 Pluto, the planet of power, fanaticism, regeneration and the body defences, moved into the 6th house of public health of the horoscope of the United States. In November 1983 Pluto moved into Scorpio, its own sign, magnifying all that is associated with the sign and planet.

In 1979, well-known American medical astrologer Mary Vohryzek, discussed the possibility of a forthcoming sexual disease epidemic in the USA. Mary was working on the twenty-year conjunction cycles of Jupiter and Saturn in relation to the horoscope of the United States. The horoscopes of continents are based on historic factors. The most commonly used horoscope for the USA is for 4 July, 1776, American Independence Day, with the Sun in Cancer and Moon in Aquarius. I personally consider the chart with Gemini Ascendant and Aquarius on the Midheaven to be the most accurate.

The United State Centers for Disease Control define AIDS as 'a disease at least moderately predictive of a defect in cell mediated immunity occurring in a person with no known cause for diminished resistance to that disease'. (*The Medical Journal of Australia* — June 11, 1983).

My own research on AIDS consists of a mere nineteen cases with complete birth data, sixteen of which were published in the American journal *Mercury Hour.* In view of what we know about AIDS, it is ridiculous to suggest that people born under certain Sun signs are more likely to contact AIDS than others. However, I will comment on the nineteen cases at my disposal.

Firstly, the Sun sign distribution was as follows:–

Aries 1, Taurus 3, Gemini nil, Cancer 2, Leo nil, Virgo 1, Libra 2, Scorpio 4, Sagittarius 1, Capricorn 1, Aquarius 2 and Pisces 2, with the largest number of placements in the Taurus/Scorpio polarity.

Examination of the full horoscopes produced further information. Using the same point system as the other illnesses in this book, the total distribution of elements in the nineteen was as follows:–

Fire 104 points, Earth 92 points, Air 113 points, and Water 128 points, which totalled 220 points to Yin signs (Earth and Water) and 217 points to Yang signs (Fire and Air).

In the case of individual distribution, many of the patients (ten of the nineteen) had evenly distributed Yin and Yang energies. Usually when there was an imbalance, it was severe: five patients had an overload of Yin signs and four had an overload of Yang signs. The distinguishing thread I found in other illnesses was missing.

Distinguishing factors in this test group

1. The Pluto/Scorpio Factor

The single-most predominant factor in this group was the Pluto/Scorpio factor, which means that the sign of Scorpio and the placement of Pluto was prominent at birth. Some cases had greater emphasis than others, but all shared this factor. As Pluto rules Scorpio and to a great extent, AIDS is a sexually transmitted disease involving the defence system, it is not an unexpected finding. Those who did not have the Sun in Scorpio frequently had the Moon, Mercury, Mars, Ascendant or Midheaven in Scorpio. Twelve of the nineteen had Pluto on the 'Angles' in their birth charts, which means rising, culminating, setting or approaching the Immum Coeli of the chart (where the lower meridian intersects the ecliptic). Planets on the angles at birth describe the type of active involvement the individual will initiate in his or her own life plus the interaction with others on the conscious and subconscious levels.

2. The Saturn and Neptune Factors

Saturn and Neptune were frequently in a hard aspect to the Sun or Ascendant in the natal chart, with the single-most common aspect being Neptune conjunction the Ascendant in five cases. However these aspects are also common factors in the horoscopes of those suffering from other illnesses. They define points of vulnerability which can lead to illnesses in some cases, depending upon diet, lifestyle and other factors. Astrology can detect the periods in the life when these points of vulnerability are activated, thus making the individual more susceptible to illness.

3. Activation — Periods of lowered resistance

The period when severe AIDS symptoms manifested coincided with classic astrological lowered resistance patterns in the horoscope of the individual. However I have observed these same astrological patterns at work in the charts of those suffering from other diseases, especially cancer, which suggest that if the person had not contacted AIDS, he or she would have been susceptible to another illness at that time.

ASTROLOGICAL RESEARCH OF ILLNESS — GENERAL

It is advisable for astrologers researching illness to call upon outside birth data in addition to that provided by their own clients for synchronicity and astrology are so closely intertwined (see Chapter 1). Two different astrologers may attract two groups of clients suffering from the same illness, but as there is usually an astrological affinity between astrologer and client, one astrologer may reach a different set of conclusions to the other. Each astrologer may have a quite different, but consistent, astrological emphasis in his or her own group of clients.

This possibility came to my attention when I attended a lecture given by an excellent astrologer/psychologist who pointed out that '70 per cent of clients who consult psychologists have very few Earth signs in their birth charts, because it is difficult for them to 'Earth' themselves'. This concept fascinated me; as the lecturer was an Earth Sun sign herself, I wondered if she was attracting low-Earth people because she could, as well as advising them, provide a first-hand 'Earthy' approach for them. It would be interesting to hear the findings of an astrologer/psychologist who has a low-Earth chart.

Those who are contemplating a research project in medical astrology are advised to read *Recent Advances in Natal Astrology,* a mammoth work by scientist and astrologer, Dr Geoffrey Dean. The book contains valuable information on statistics and perspectives plus a vast record of past astrological research. It approaches the practice of astrology from a modern scientific viewpoint which may sting the belief system of many astrologers.

However, the work I have done in astrology over a period of nearly twenty years confirms many of the findings of the astrologers before me. As medical astrology can be of assistance to humanity, the advent of the computer age should enable us to eliminate the superstitions and outdated theories and concentrate on relevant facts which can be useful in diagnosis and prevention. But it is important to bear in mind that astrology is an area dealing with people, their emotions and feelings and, as such, is a subjective study which is difficult to scientifically prove or disprove.

Chapter Thirteen

Astro-Hereditary Aspects —
The Astrological Family Tree

We have all observed common birth signs and sometimes common birth dates within a family. Is this mere coincidence or are there astro-hereditary threads which can be linked to personality traits and inherited characteristics, such as a predisposition to a specific illness?

As outlined in Chapter 1, French psychologist Michel Gauquelin observed that a high frequency of particular planets were rising and culminating at the time of birth of groups of people working in the same profession. Gauquelin also observed that it was not unusual for the same planet to be prominent at the birth time of their children. It therefore follows that if the planets can be linked to personality traits and human characteristics, they can be linked to a hereditary factor.

My own research has confirmed that there is a repetition of zodiac signs and planetary patterns in families. These patterns give the astrologer some idea of the vulnerable body areas. In addition, it can be seen which patterns and signs are 'inherited' from a particular side of the family. Sometimes a planetary pattern will appear in a family member, miss a generation, then reppear in the grandchild. I can trace a planetary pattern in my own birth chart back to my grandfather on my mother's side of the family. The pattern has not reappeared in any other family member since then.

Some may ask if it is possible to use astrology to trace parentage and my answer would be that it has distinct possibilities. If the astrologer had the birth charts of three adults and a child and two of the adults had parented the child, there should be adequate astrological links between parents and child to eliminate one of the adults as a blood relative.

COMPATIBILITY IN RELATIONSHIPS

Astrology is a valuable guide when assessing the compatibility of two people in a relationship. All successful relationships require effort by both parties, but some have less conflict than others. Comparison of the astrological charts demonstrates the areas of ease, but also the areas of work required to keep the relationship alive and ongoing. There is no such thing as a perfect match.

When two strangers meet and a special attraction exists, there are always astrological links between the two horoscopes. The two people may eventually marry and although they are not 'blood' relatives, they share astrological family patterns which will eventually recur in the horoscopes of their children or in later generations. This is demonstrated in this chapter. Certain astrological degrees in the horoscopes of Princess Diana and Sarah, the Duchess of York are compared with other members of the English royal family.

Saturn/Uranus Combinations
The Richardson Family
Andrew Richardson was born in 1940, when Saturn and Uranus were in conjunction in the heavens. His first daughter Marina, was born in 1964 when Saturn and Uranus were in opposition, and his second daughter Anna was born in 1975, when Saturn was in square, or 90-degrees to Uranus.

In the birth horoscope, 'action' connections between Saturn and Uranus endow the individual with a remarkable determination and a capacity to 'break new ground'. Such individuals are often highly creative in their chosen field. George Gershwin, whose music still enjoys world wide popularity, was born in 1898, when Saturn and Uranus were within 7-degrees of a conjunction to each other and to Gershwin's Ascendant. Andrew Richardson was a professional musician for twenty years and his daughters both have a natural aptitude for music.

But Saturn/Uranus combinations can also act like a pressure cooker. Uranus energy must be free to express itself and Saturn energy blocks the expression. Uranus eventually breaks down the resistance and subsequent action is often sudden and unexpected. Saturn/Uranus people are frequently tense and it is important for them to find a safety valve through activities such as dance or sport, thus enabling them to release their tensions and avoid an accumulation of pressure. As can be expected, Saturn/Uranus people often suffer from stress and fluctuating blood pressure.

George Gershwin died unexpectedly of a brain tumour shortly before he was thirty-nine years of age. The fact that the Sat-
urn/Uranus conjunction was so close to his natal Ascendant,
made the conjunction more significant to his physical body than
to the thousands of other people born on the same day. Andrew
Richardson's father died suddenly of a cerebral haemorrhage
when Andrew was 31 years old. Most Saturn/Uranus people
devise their own personal formula for venting this dynamic force
by recognising their needs and finding a suitable outlet for their
tensions and creativity.

In *The Combination of Stellar Influences*, Reinhold Ebertin
describes the biological correspondences of Saturn/Uranus as
'inhibitions of rhythm, heart-block, unrhythmical processes,
sudden removal of an intestinal part'.

Saturn/Uranus conjunctions occur at approximately forty-
five-year intervals and in recent years have occurred in 1897,
1941/42 and 1988. Saturn/Uranus oppositions occurred in
1918/1919 and between 1964 and 1966.

The innovative musician Paul McCartney was born on 18
June, 1942 when Saturn was conjunction to Uranus. He was at
the peak of his success in 1964, when Saturn and Uranus were in
opposition. His music enjoyed renewed success in 1988, when
Saturn and Uranus completed a cycle and formed another conjunction.

It can be seen above that like all planetary patterns,
Saturn/Uranus combinations have both positive and negative
expressions. There is no single planetary combination in the
heavens which is purely positive or purely negative.

UNEXPLAINABLE COINCIDENCES

The Ascendant and Midheaven are the fastest-moving points in
the birth horoscope. An accurate birth-time is required to calcu-
late these points, which are adjusted for the place of birth. The
Ascendant, or 'rising sign', changes rapidly at the rate of approximately one-degree every four minutes. A complete zodiac sign
takes roughly two hours to rise, but accurate calculations are
required for exact measurements. Most Western astrologers use
the tropical zodiac for their calculations. In the example below

I have referred to the Ascendant and Midheaven as the 'time-of-birth' degrees.

The placement of the Sun in the zodiac changes at the rate of approximately one-degree per day, and it takes about thirty days for the Sun to move through a complete zodiac sign. I have referred to the Sun degree below as the 'day-of-birth' degree.

The Richardson Family — further astro-hereditary links

Marina, the eldest daughter of the Richardson family, was born on 8 July 1964. Her Sun position is 16 degrees, 12 minutes of Cancer. Her father Andrew, is a Leo but his fast-moving Ascendant degree, based on an accurate birth time from hospital records, is 16 degrees, 16 minutes of Cancer. Coincidence? Marina's fast-moving Ascendant degree, based on an accurate birth time recorded by her mother Barbara at Marina's birth, is 6 degrees, 33 minutes of Aquarius. When Barbara was born many years before, 6 degrees, 32 minutes of Aquarius was on the Midheaven. The Midheaven is the second fast-moving point in the birth horoscope. In other words ...

- Marina's 'day-of-birth' degree (her Sun degree) was at the same position as one of her father's 'time-of-birth' degrees (Andrew's Ascendant);
- Marina's 'time-of-birth' degree (Ascendant) was at the same position as her mother's second 'time-of-birth' degree (Barbara's Midheaven).

Marina had 'inherited' her father's nurturing trait (Cancer) and her mother's intellectual, humanitarian trait (Aquarius). In adult life Marina became a nursing sister.

The Richardson story may sound conveniently accurate, but I know the family well and have personally researched the birth times — accurate birth times are essential in a study such as this. The chance of a random link-up of the fast-moving degrees of three people born in different years would be minimal, but working with astrology daily, I see these family 'coincidences' often and know them to be consistent. (Figure 9 illustrates the astro-hereditary links of three members of the Richardson family.) Even after so many years in astrology I am still in awe to find such order and sequence in the lives of human beings. Some authorities suggest that astrology can drive a person away from

God, but astrology can in fact, make us aware that there is a force
at work far greater than humble humans can ever hope to equal.
Call it God, Nature or the Universal Force.

ANDREW RICHARDSON (father)—— BARBARA RICHARDSON (mother)

ASCENDANT 16°16' CANCER   MIDHEAVEN 6°32' AQUARIUS
(fast-moving point)   (fast-moving point)

            MARINA RICHARDSON (daughter)

            SUN 16°12' CANCER
            ASCENDANT 6°33' AQUARIUS (fast-moving point)

Figure 9: *Astro-Hereditary Links – The Richardson Family*

THE ENGLISH ROYAL FAMILY

Figure 10 illustrates a simple astrological family tree of zodiac
signs found in the horoscopes of the English royal family. It
includes the Sun signs, Moon signs and Ascendant and Midheav-
en signs where a birth-time is available. The royal family is an
excellent case study because when birth-times are available they
are widely publicised and accurate. I have included as many family members as space allows.

It can be seen that certain zodiac signs are highlighted, name-
ly the Taurus/Scorpio polarity, Cancer and Leo.

Taurus/Scorpio

Queen Elizabeth II was born on 21 April, 1926 when the Sun was
at 0 degrees, 12 minutes of Taurus. When her son Prince Charles
was born, the Moon was at 0 degrees, 26 minutes of Taurus. The
Moon returns to this degree in the zodiac every 27 days 7 hours
43 minutes and 11.5 seconds. The variation between the Sun
degree of the Queen and the Moon degree of Prince Charles can
be measured in minutes.

At the birth of Prince Charles' son William, Jupiter was at
0 degrees, 29 minutes of Scorpio, opposite the shared point of

the Queen and Prince Charles. At the birth of Prince Henry,
Pluto was at 0 degrees, 34 minutes of Scorpio.

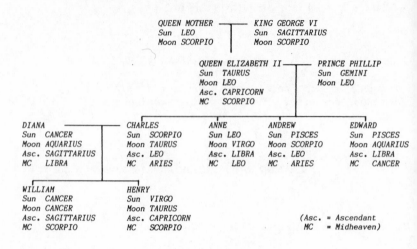

Figure 10: *The Astrological Family Tree – English Royal Family*

Other Significant Astrological Connections

Below is a list of zodiac degrees which feature in the horoscopes
of members of the royal family. The list includes Princess Diana
and Sarah, Duchess of York, who married into the royal family.

TAURUS/SCORPIO

21 degrees, 22 minutes Taurus	... Prince Henry's Moon.
24 degrees, 25 minutes Taurus	... Princess Diana's Venus.
25 degrees, 39 minutes Taurus	... Prince William's Venus.
17 degrees, 08 minutes, Scorpio	... Prince Henry's Midheaven.
18 degrees, 15 minutes, Scorpio	... Sarah, Duchess of York's Ascendant.
22 degrees, 25 minutes, Scorpio	... Prince Charles' Sun.
25 degrees, 37 minutes, Scorpio	... Queen Elizabeth II's Midheaven.
25 degrees, 30 minutes, Scorpio	... Prince Andrew's Moon.

CANCER

0 degrees, 06 minutes, Cancer	... Prince William's Sun.
1 degrees, 30 minutes, Cancer	... Princess Beatrice's Venus.
3 degrees, 12 minutes, Cancer	... Princess Diana's Mercury.
4 degrees, 54 minutes, Cancer	... Princess Beatrice's Moon.

4 degrees, 57 minutes, Cancer	... Prince William's Moon.
9 degrees, 40 minutes, Cancer	... Princess Diana's Sun.

LEO

5 degrees, 27 minutes, Leo	... Prince Charles' Ascendant.
11 degrees, 36 minutes, Leo	... Prince Andrew's Ascendant.
11 – 12 degrees, Leo	... Queen Mother's Sun (birth-time unknown).
12 degrees, 07 minutes, Leo	... Queen Elizabeth II's Moon.
16 degrees, 26 minutes, Leo	... Princess Beatrice's Sun.

In the royal family 'tree' there are other shared zodiac signs and degrees, but these examples should adequately demonstrate my point.

Sensitive health areas
From the thread of the Taurus, Scorpio, Cancer and Leo in the royal family tree, it can be seen that the heart, back, digestion, throat, certain glands, the immune and reproductive systems are the prominent hereditary health patterns in the royal family. They are known for their interest in correct nutrition and it is not surprising to hear that their awareness and utilisation of natural foods and remedies has been passed down from one generation to the next.

Inherited planetary patterns
There are many interesting planetary patterns in the astrological family tree of the royal family similar to the Saturn/Uranus combinations of the Richardson family. I have not included a comprehensive diagram of the planetary patterns as it may prove confusing to the layperson, but a few patterns are listed below:–

SATURN/NEPTUNE
Saturn opposition Neptune (Queen Mother)
Saturn square (90-degrees from) Neptune (Queen Elizabeth II)
Saturn semi-square (45 degrees from) Neptune (Prince Henry)

SUN/MARS
Sun conjunction Mars (Prince Phillip)
Sun conjunction Mars (Prince Edward)

Sun conjunction Mars (Sarah Duchess of York)
Sun square Mars (Prince Henry)

SUN/SATURN
Sun sesquiquadrate (135 degrees from) Saturn – (Queen Mother)
Sun square Saturn (Prince Phillip)
Sun semi-square Saturn (Prince Andrew)
Sun semi-square Saturn (Prince Henry).

There are many other planetary patterns traceable through the royal family. Each pattern gives clues as to family health factors.

The Saturn/Neptune patterns often produce deeply religious traits. The person usually has a deep compassion for the less fortunate, but there is frequently personal suffering through the behaviour of others.

The Sun/Mars patterns relate to muscles, cells and heart. Most Sun/Mars people are gregarious and have a strong life force.

The Sun/Saturn combinations suggest areas of sluggishness, calcification and stiffness of the body. Sun/Saturn people are usually reserved and dignified.

It is interesting that Prince Phillip and Prince Henry both have Sun/Mars and Sun/Saturn combinations, which indicates they would be tireless and determined workers who are usually in full control, but who are occasionally prone to energetic outbursts. Such a combination favours sporting pursuits which require a high level of endurance.

Rectification of the Birth Horoscope
Rectification of the birth horoscope is an advanced technique used by astrologers to establish the correct birth time for a person whose birth time is unknown. It involves listing significant life events and working backwards towards the birth-time; hereditary zodiac signs and planetary patterns play an important role in rectification. In her book *Cosmobiology: A Modern Approach to Astrology*, renowned Australian astrologer Doris Greaves, who pioneered many aspects of astrology in Australia, examines a family tree and establishes a correct birth time for one of the family members.

Chapter Fourteen

Additional Interpretation of Case Studies

This chapter is designed for those who have done some astrological study. A simplified level of interpretation has been maintained and only relevant points have been highlighted. You may enjoy adding your own interpretation to mine.

PRINCESS DIANA OF ENGLAND

Figure 11: Cosmobiology chart including solar arc progressions and secondary progressed full Moon placement for August 1987. (From Chapter 5, 'The Phases of the Moon'.)

Diana was born on 1 July, 1961, with the Sun in Cancer and Moon in Aquarius, when the Moon was within 18 minutes of orb of its exact disseminating phase. Despite the orb, Diana undoubtedly displays the crusading qualities of the disseminating type, which is reinforced by Uranus semi-square Sun, square Venus and opposition Moon in her natal chart. She is highly effective in her role as a world trendsetter.

During her secondary progressed full Moon cycle, which became exact in August 1987, Diana would have found it difficult to ignore the inner conflict aroused through her new awareness. Frequently the progressed full Moon coincides with a strong desire to separate from existing conditions and explore new modes of expression.

The magic of the 90-degree work dial beautifully illustrates the degree of the progressed full Moon (4.31 Aquarius/Leo) on Diana's natal Jupiter in Aquarius (= high expectations, an over-optimistic attitude towards partnerships). In addition, the progressed full Moon activates the dynamic 45-degree aspects to the progressed Sun (Sun=Moon=Venus=Uranus), via the solar arc progressions. This tendency is exaggerated by the progression of Saturn by solar arc, to Diana's natal Sun=Moon=Venus=Uranus syndrome.

It is interesting that Prince Charles has his natal Ascendant at 5.27 Leo. As Diana's progressed full Moon occurred within one

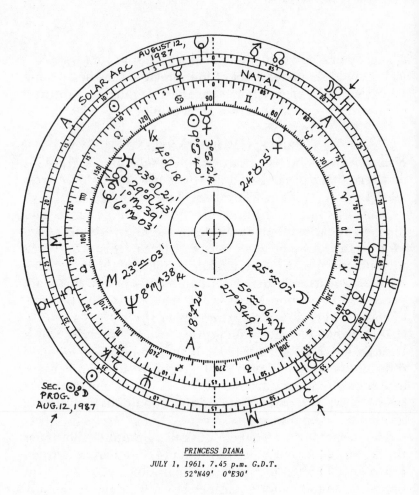

PRINCESS DIANA

JULY 1, 1961, 7.45 p.m. G.D.T.
52°N49' 0°E30'

Figure 11: *Princess Diana of England – Cosmobiology Chart*

degree of Charles' Ascendant/Descendant axis, it can be seen, even without assessing Charles' full horoscope, that Diana's personal tests and challenges would involve him. It will be remembered that Diana's progressed full Moon cycle coincided with her well-publicised period of restlessness and marital friction.

WILLIAM LILLY

Figure 12: Cosmobiology natal chart interfaced with the transitting planetary positions for the commencement of the Great Fire of London. (From Chapter 10, 'World Health Cycles'.)

William Lilly was born on 1 May, 1602 in Leicester, England. He was the astrologer who successfully predicted the Great Plague and Great Fire of London. Because I do not have Lilly's birth time I have calculated the planetary positions for noon on his date of birth. The Ascendant and Midheaven, which rely on an accurate birth time, have been deleted.

As in the case of Louis Pasteur, William Lilly's horoscope demonstrates a capacity to 'earth' the intellect, inspiration and psychic intuition. The Sun in Taurus conjunction to Mercury, Venus and Uranus means radical and restless thinking, accelerated mental vibrations, flashes of intuition and genius, an aptitude for mathematics, science and music. The German system of cosmobiology uses direct and indirect midpoints. Lilly's natal Sun/Mercury/Venus/Uranus conjunction forms an indirect midpoint to Mars and Jupiter, denoting success through his mental faculties.

On the day the Great Fire of London commenced, (2 September, 1666), Venus was square to Saturn in the heavens, which activated Lilly's natal Jupiter semi-square Neptune aspect (= changeable environment, fluctuating financial circumstances, profit through loss and speculation). The Mars/Pluto (violent force and energy) aspect on the day of the fire, was placed in the midpoint of Lilly's Sun/Uranus/Mercury/Venus conjunction and Saturn (= a mental and physical crisis, separations and loss as a result of violent energy and higher forces, sudden accidents.) Even without an accurate birth time, it can be seen that the events of 2 September had an extremely traumatic effect on Lilly. The heavy involvement of Saturn suggests feelings of responsibility, conscience and deep personal soul-searching.

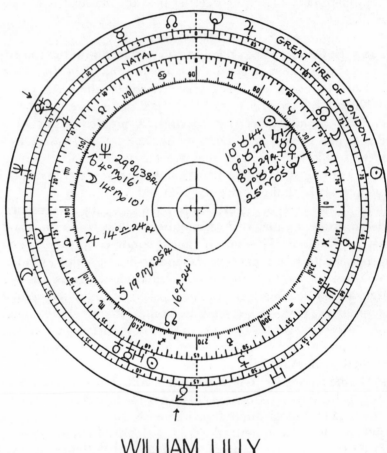

WILLIAM LILLY
May 1, 1602

Figure 12:
William Lilly – Cosmobiology Natal Chart interfaced with Great Fire of London

DR JONAS SALK

Figure 13: Traditional natal chart (From Chapter 10, 'World Health Cycles'.)

Born on 28 October, 1914, Dr Salk is the world-famous creator of the Salk vaccine. His natal horoscope shows him to be a man of magnificent obsessions, a person of power and ingenuity. With the Sun, Ascendant, Mercury and Mars in Scorpio, plus a dominant 8th house, his determination to overcome obstacles and improve the quality of human life would be his major motivating force. Dr Salk would have a bulldog quality, a courage to fight for his convictions and hold on when others have given up (eight placements in fixed signs including Mercury conjunction Mars in Scorpio).

The 'T-square' between the Sun, Uranus and Neptune suggests a unique personality, with almost psychic intuition, an inventor with definite ideas. The grand trine in Water signs between the Sun, Moon and Pluto, is reinforced through its placement in the Water houses. Dr Salk may perceive this as a spiritual destiny to humanity and use his abilities to transform the lives of the families around him. Although it may not always be possible, he would enjoy working alone. From the perspective of health, his chart suggests a significant link to the immune system, possibly giving him an instinctive understanding of this function.

HELENE

Cancer case study — *Figure 14*: Traditional natal chart (From Chapter 12, 'The Onset of Illness'.)

Helene was born on 19 January, 1929 at 3.30 p.m. in Amsterdam, Holland. She became ill with cancer in 1985 and had her breast removed in July of that year. The cancer recurred and by March 1986 was present in her lungs, bones and head. She did not survive her illness.

As discussed in 'The Onset of Illness', Helene has the classic overload of Earth and Water in her chart with only Saturn and Uranus in Fire signs. The overload of Yin signs (17 points) against the 6 points of her Yang signs, strengthens her tendency to internalise rather than externalise her life expressions.

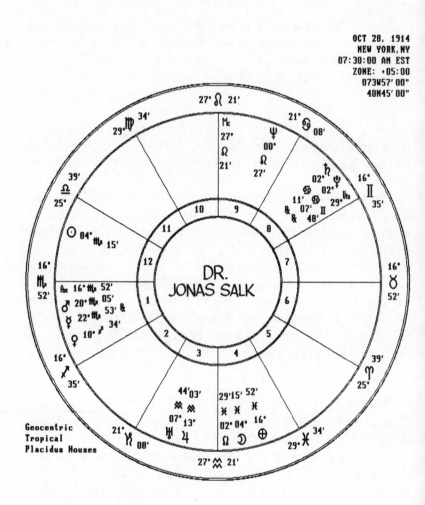

Figure 13: *Dr Jonas Salk – Traditional Natal Chart*

As a Capricorn Sun sign person with a Cancer Ascendant conjunct Pluto, Helene is shown as an intensely emotional, almost obsessive personality, with a great attachment to her home and children, but unsettling circumstances are indicated in the family structure. Helene in fact bore six children and when her husband was unexpectedly killed in an accident, she reared the children single-handedly, while working full-time and studying at night to improve her career prospects. There is no doubt that Helene was a woman of conviction and courage.

The sign of Cancer rules the breasts and Capricorn rules the bones. Saturn (bones and calcification) in the 6th house of health, is opposition Mars in the 12th house of institutions. The pattern suggests an ability to work hard in service to others, but is undermining to the general health. The individual can suffer from highly fluctuating energy levels, mixed enthusiasm and destructive or blocked expressions of energy.

In *The Combination of Stellar Influences*, Reinhold Ebertin describes the biological correspondence of the Mars/Saturn energy as ...

> *'The bone-forming processes, joints, muscles as active factors and bones as passive factors, an inflammation of the bones or of the bone-marrow, the death or atrophy of an organ, a paralysis of muscles belonging to the breathing mechanism.'*

Activation of Helene's horoscope

At the time of Helene's operation in July 1985, her natal Sun in Capricorn had progressed to 25 degrees, 51 minutes, of Pisces, which was exactly square to her natal Saturn in the 6th house of health. The progressed Sun had activated the destructive energy pattern associated with muscle and bone. But the approach of the progressed Sun to this point would have become increasingly effective over the two-year period prior to the operation. In Helene's birth chart, the natal Sun was in square to the natal Saturn/Neptune (health midpoint), suggesting a propensity towards lingering illnesses. In this case, when progressed Sun squared natal Saturn, it involved a severe health test.

At 0 degrees, 04 minutes of Capricorn, the secondary progressed Saturn, which moves much slower than the progressed Sun, had changed sign and formed a grand Earth trine with

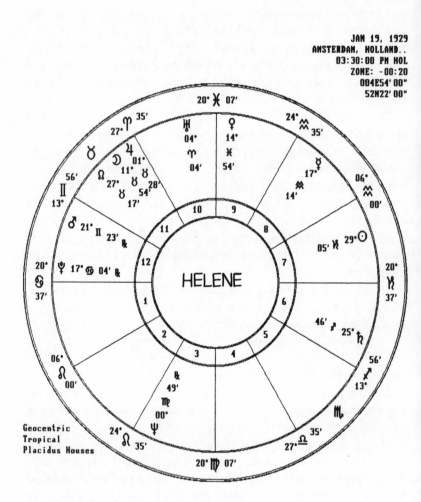

Figure 14: *Cancer Case Study – Helene's Horoscope*

natal Neptune in the 3rd house and natal Jupiter in the 11th house. Whilst a grand tine is generally considered favourable and highly creative, it can also generate unrealistic expectations and a diffusion of energy. I believe at this stage, Helene's spirituality gained depth and sustenance.

Another astrological technique which displays amazing accuracy and which is popular with cosmobiologists, is that of solar arc progression, in which all the progressed planets and points are moved symbolically at the rate of the Sun. During July 1985, solar arc Venus at 11 degrees, 49 minutes Taurus was conjunct the natal Moon position of 11 degrees, 54 minutes Taurus. Venus and the Moon connected to become heavily involved in the astrological health theme for that year. The Venus/Moon connection described by Dr Schwab had been made. (See Chapter 12, 'The Onset of Illness'.)

Amongst other things, the transits for July 1985 indicate that the Sun and Mars formed an exact conjunction at 25 degrees, 20 minutes Cancer on 18 July. In the period immediately prior to this date, the Sun and Mars had both transitted Helene's natal Ascendant at 20 degrees, 38 minutes of Cancer, a classic astrological pattern for an operation or other high-energy event involving the physical body of the individual.

GRAHAM

Figure 15: **Kidney Transplant Case Study** — Year of first transplant (From Chapter 12, 'The Onset of Illness'.)

Graham is the patient with the two unsuccessful kidney transplants, referred to in 'The Onset of Illness'. The graphic illustration (Figure 15) was originated in Germany by Reinhold Ebertin. The Australian version for current years is produced by my own academy, the Australian Academy of Astrology and Cosmobiology. Firstly the graph outlines the planetary patterns operating in a specific year, in this case 1976, and their mathematical relationship to the patterns which existed at Graham's birth and which I have drawn on as horizontal lines. The technique is known as transit comparison and is based on the premise that the individual is psychically aware of his or her own placement in the universal order of things. When the current planet placements coincide with the natal zodiac degrees, or

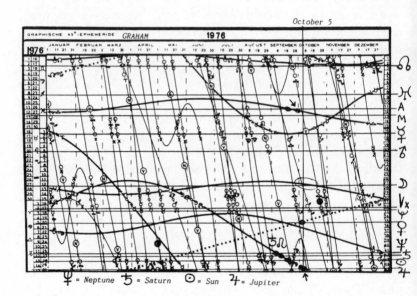

Figure 15: *45-degree Transit Graph for first Kidney Transplant – Graham*

form an aspect to them, the person will experience the energies associated with the planets in question. It is an effective guide and an easy technique to test, so it is surprising that it can be so easily overlooked by non-astrologers merely because its effectiveness cannot be explained in scientific terms.

Graham was born with the Sun in Pisces in opposition to Neptune. The Jupiter/Saturn conjunction in Taurus formed 45-degree and 135-degree aspects to the Sun and Neptune respectively, which places the four points together on the 45-degree graphic ephemeris. Graham has the Moon in Sagittarius, an Aries Ascendant and Capricorn on the Midheaven. Despite the obvious strengths in the chart, the over-riding sensitivity of the Pisces Sun reinforced by its opposition to Neptune, makes Graham a vulnerable candidate for illness, prone to allergies and drug sensitivity.

Graham's first donor kidney was from a non-living cadaver and this transplant was carried out on 5 October, 1976. Unfortunately the transplant was conducted under difficult astrological conditions, although the conditions themselves may have contributed to the necessity of the operation. The first transplant occurred towards the end of a period of approximately one month when Saturn (limitation, depression, slow recovery) was activating the birth Saturn/Neptune/Sun/Jupiter pattern. The one-month period leading up to the operation would have resulted in a particularly low physical and mental ebb for Graham leaving him in a depleted state.

On the day of the first transplant operation on 5 October, 1976, the Sun was in Libra (kidneys), conjunction to Pluto and opposition Graham's natal Ascendant in Aries (= transformation in the life of the individual, through the intervention of another). Although the transitting Jupiter was in a wide square to his natal Mercury (hope and faith), its softer sextile aspects to the natal Sun and Pluto and trine to the natal Neptune did not provide adequate protection. I have drawn a vertical line on the graph for the date of the first transplant operation.

The failed kidney was removed on 9 November, 1976. The second transplant was performed on 6 June, 1977 and this time the donor was a living blood relative. Transitting Saturn had retrograded bàck over the vulnerable Saturn/Neptune/Sun/Jupiter aspect pattern during January and February, and by May and June had moved back to where it had been at the time of the first unsuccessful transplant. The restricting, depressing, slow-recovery factor of Saturn would have once again hindered Graham's chance of being physically and emotionally equipped to deal with the second transplant. In addition, Pluto had returned to its opposition to the Ascendant and once again the favourable indicators were overshadowed by the limiting factors.

Conclusion

If the reader has gained some new perspectives and personal enlightenment through this work, then I have succeeded in my objectives. If you wish to pursue astrology further, there are many ethical people practising astrology throughout the world and if the time is right, the law of synchronicity will guide you to them.

Astrology can never be dismissed as superstition by those who have approached it seriously and with humility. Rather than adopting a fixed opinion, armchair critics would do well to look beyond its popular presentation and investigate the subject with an open mind. As I pointed out many times in this work, astrology is a subjective science and as such, is difficult to assess under an objective criterion. But I have yet to read any convincing evidence which would alter my opinion as to its value and effectiveness.

Further Reading

Andrews, Allan, *Quotations for Speakers and Writers*, Pan, London

Arroyo, Stephen, *Astrology, Karma and Transformation*, CRCS Publications, Post Office Drawer 4307, Vancouver, Washington 98662, USA

Barnhart, Clarence L. & Barnhart, Robert K., *The World Book Dictionary*, World Book Inc., USA

Bizony, M.T. (ed.) *The New Space Encyclopaedia*, Artemis Press, Horsham, Sussex

Bradley, Donald A., *Solar and Lunar Returns*, Llewellyn, St Paul, Minnesota

Brau, Jean-Louis, Weaver, Helen, & Edmands, Allan, *Larousse Encyclopedia of Astrology*, New American Library, New York

Dean, Dr Geoffrey, *Recent Advances in Natal Astrology*, The Astrological Association, 36 Tweedy Road, Bromley, Kent BR1 3PP, England

De Vore, Nicholas, *Encyclopedia of Astrology*, Littlefield, Adams & Co., Totowa, New Jersey

Ebertin, Reinhold, *The Combination of Stellar Influences*, Ebertin Verlag, Wurttemberg, West Germany

Fekete, Irene & Ward, Peter Dorrington, *Disease and Medicine*, Orbis Publishing, London

Gauquelin, Michel, *The Truth About Astrology*, Basil Blackwell, Oxford

Gauquelin, Michel, *The Cosmic Clocks*, Avon Books, New York

Gawler, Ian, *You Can Conquer Cancer*, Hill of Content, Melbourne

Geddes, Sheila, *Astrology and Health*, Thorsons, Wellingborough

George, Llewellyn, *A to Z Horoscope Maker & Delineator*, Llewellyn, Saint Paul, Minnesota

Gibran, Kahlil, *The Wisdom of Gibran*, Philosophical Library, New York

Greaves, Doris E., *Cosmobiology: A Modern Approach to Astrology*, Regulus Astrological Publications, Tathra, NSW 2550, Australia

Greene, Liz, *The Astrology of Fate*, Allen and Unwin, London

Health & Living, Glenfield, Auckland, May 1989

Hyman, Robin, *A Dictionary of Famous Quotations*, Pan Books, London

Jansky, Robert Carl, *Astrology, Nutrition & Health*, Para Research, Rockport, Massachusetts

Jones, M.E., *Sabian Symbols in Astrology*, Shambhala Press, Boulder, Colorado

Kenton, Warren, *Astrology, the Celestial Mirror*, Saracen Books, Sydney

Kimmel, Eleonora, *Patterns of Destiny*, American Federation of Astrologers, PO Box 22040, 6535 South Rural Road, Tempe, AZ 85282, USA

Kimmel, Eleonora, *Cosmobiology Journal*, Cosmobiological Research Foundation, PO Box 10631, Denver, CO 80210, USA

Mercury Hour, C-7 3509 Waterlick Road, Lynchburg, VA 24502, USA, July 1989

Michelsen, Neil F., *The American Ephemeris for the 20th Century, 1990 to 2000*, ACS Publications, PO Box 16430, San Diego, CA 92116-0430, USA

Michelsen, Neil F., *The American Ephemeris for the 21st Century, 2001 to 2050*, ACS Publications, San Diego, USA

Mountfield, Anne, *Looking Back at Medicine*, Macmillan Education, Basingstoke, Hampshire

Muirden, James, *Astronomy Handbook*, Kingfisher Books, London

Nauman, Eileen, *The American Book of Nutrition and Medical Astrology*, Astro
   Computing Services, PO Box 16430, San Diego, California, USA

Nesle, Solange de Mailly, *Astrology*, Inner Traditions International, New York

Ostrander, Sheila, & Schroeder, Lynn, *Natural Birth Control*, Bantam Books,
   New York

Peat, F. David, *Synchronicity: The Bridge Between Matter and the Mind*, Bantam,
   New York

Petulengro, *Herbs, Health and Astrology*, Keats Publishing, New Canaan,
   Connecticut

Police Life, Box 2763Y, GPO Melbourne, Victoria 3001, October 1984

Rodden, Lois M., *The American Book of Charts*, Astro Computing Services,
   PO Box 16430, San Diego, CA 92116, USA

Rodden, Lois M., *Profiles of Women*, The American Federation of Astrologers,
   PO Box 22040, Tempe, AZ 85285-2040, USA

Rudhyar, Dane, *The Lunation Cycle*, Aurora Press, New York

Simmonite, W.J. & Culpeper, N., *The Simmonite-Culpeper Herbal Remedies*,
   Universal Publishing, New York

Townley, John, *Astrological Life Cycles*, Destiny Books, New York

Willson, Robina Beckles, *Anna Pavloca — A Legend Among Dancers*, Hodder and
   Stoughton, Sevenoaks, Kent

YOUR PERSONAL HOROSCOPE PRINTOUT

If you wish to have a complete list of your Ascendant,
Midheaven and planetary positions at birth, to use
with this book, you can apply to the:
Australian Academy of Astrology & Cosmobiology,
P.O. Box 27, Burwood, 3125, Victoria, Australia.